Coming Up on Your Left

A Tour Guide's Guidebook

Happy Trails!

Joemy Wilson

Joemy Wilson

With a Foreword by Ted Bravos

JourneyWoman Press

Published by JourneyWoman Press

Copyright © 2013 by Joemy Wilson

For all inquiries, please contact:
journeywomanpress@gmail.com

Cover photograph by Jon Harvey

ISBN: 0615831044
ISBN 13: 9780615831046

Printed in the United States of America

For Jon, my very favorite guide

CONTENTS

———

FOREWORD

———

The moment Joemy Wilson walked into my ITMI classroom in 1999, I could tell from her smile and the sparkle in her eyes that she had the qualities that would make her an excellent tour director and guide. In the following weeks, she proved to be an outstanding student. I was not at all surprised when Tauck, one of the oldest and most respected tour companies in the world, hired her the day after graduation! Nor am I surprised now that Joemy's empathy for others and the generosity she has always shown in sharing her knowledge has inspired her to write this delightful and informative gem of a guide.

This "guidebook for guides" is a powerhouse of tour-guide tips, jam-packed with anecdotes from Joemy's extensive travels around the world as a professional tour director and guide. Some of the stories will make you laugh out loud. A few others might cause you to wipe away a tear. All of them illustrate the qualities that make a great guide and support the book's main thesis, which parallels our philosophy at ITMI: *tour directors and guides can be powerful cultural ambassadors of good will.* They can make a difference in how people view the world by promoting greater understanding and respect for diversity and culture through thoughtful and meaningful travel.

Serving as a cultural good-will ambassador is an enormous responsibility. Joemy Wilson takes this responsibility seriously, but with an infectious sense of fun. Just read the Table of Contents, for example, and you'll see what I mean… *If You're Gonna Rob the Stagecoach, Don't Ride Your Own Horse…*don't you just want to read it right now?

As any travel guidebook should be, this one is exceptionally well organized. Each chapter illustrates an important trait of a remarkable tour guide. Special factors that apply to city motor-coach tours, walking excursions, and multi-day journeys are covered with wit and wisdom. Joemy shares three simple rules that serve as useful memory pegs to hang information on, driving home the important lessons of this book.

Coming Up on Your Left brilliantly explains how to cultivate your innate potential as an ambassador of good will wherever you guide. It illustrates how you can help transform lives by facilitating emotional connections between people of different cultures, helping them to understand and respect diversity – how you can turn a tourist into a traveler, a trip into a journey, a travel moment into a lifetime memory. It gives you the tools to become the best guide you can be!

In 1976, I co-founded the International Tour Management Institute (ITMI), the premier institute for the training and certification of tour directors and guides. The institute's intensive 15-day training program has certified over 7,000 individuals from all walks of life – people who have a passion for travel and who want to make a difference in the lives of others by showing them the wonders of our world.

Successful tour directors and guides come from amazingly diverse backgrounds. I have taught and mentored former Peace Corps volunteers, ex-military personnel, brand-new college graduates, empty nesters, and retirees. We have proudly granted ITMI certification to teachers, actors, musicians, travel agents, therapists, chefs, nurses, and hundreds of professionals from the corporate world yearning for an exciting and deeply fulfilling career where they have the freedom to chart their own course.

Joemy Wilson is an excellent example of the entrepreneurial spirit that tour directors and guides must possess to be successful. Before I met Joemy she was already an accomplished musician, having recorded numerous cutting-edge CDs in the emerging field of Celtic Music and founded her own record company. Tour directing and guiding let her combine her passion for travel and new adventures with the freedom to chart her own course.

Like most everyone we accept into the ITMI training program, Joemy already had the people skills, leadership ability, organizational skills, problem-solving skills, and something that we cannot train in class…common sense! Joemy bubbles over with a joy for life! As you read this book, you will understand more about this remarkable woman.

Each year Joemy would return to ITMI after leading tours around the world, full of enthusiasm and new stories, which she eagerly passed on to the students. For the past decade, I have had the privilege of "team teaching" with Joemy whenever she was not "on the road" leading her fellow travelers. I always love hearing her illustrate the ITMI curriculum with her own experiences and anecdotes from the road, firing up the students with the sheer joy of sharing her insights. Now she has distilled the most important of these insights and the most illuminating of the anecdotes into this delicious little guidebook. *Coming Up on Your Left: A Tour Guide's Guidebook* is a great journey with a great guide. I know you will enjoy the ride.

Ted Bravos, President and C.E.O., ITMI
San Francisco, 2013
www.itmitourtraining.com

PREFACE

————

As a tour director, I've taken travelers on fabulous vacations all over the world. The tour director's job is to make everything run as smoothly as possible, or at least to give the impression that it's all going according to plan. (It seldom is.)

I've worked with local guides in countries across the globe. The local tour guide's job is to love and know her assigned territory, and to tell wonderful stories about it – stories that entertain, inform, and inspire. She must give the impression that she can't wait to do so, even though she's done that city tour fifty-two times and counting. (Or has never done it before and is shaking in her smartly polished shoes.)

Sometimes the tour director also serves as tour guide. I've delivered local commentary from the motor coach, on ships, ferries, trains, trams, horse carriages, and on foot, from Austria to Zimbabwe. I've given city tours in Zurich, Helsinki, Vienna, Munich, Moscow, New York, Newport, Boston, Johannesburg, and many other burgs large and small.

I began my career as a local guide in Los Angeles. My first assignment, on a gorgeous day in 1998, was a standard Los Angeles city tour – Downtown, Wilshire Boulevard,

Beverly Hills, and Hollywood. I hadn't had much training, but I loved my adopted city and hoped that enthusiasm would see me through.

I was a nervous wreck through the whole thing. Traffic was jammed on the 101 Freeway and the boring bits of Wilshire, so I had to use every bit of L.A. trivia I could think of as filler. Was any of it remotely interesting? Or was everybody asleep?

Then, of course, on the Sunset Strip, traffic just zipped along. What a disaster! I didn't even have time to point out all the landmarks that were whizzing by, let alone tell the group all the fascinating Hollywood history I'd memorized so carefully. *They must hate me!* I was sure I'd missed at least a couple of major buildings on both sides of the Strip and was wondering if it was too late to go to law school when we arrived at the corner of La Brea and Hollywood Boulevard, at the Gateway.

I adore this sculpture. It's bright and shiny and over the top, pure Tinseltown, totally Hollywood. But it's also meaningful as a symbol of multi-cultural Los Angeles. As a landmark, it also meant – thank goodness! – that we were nearly back at the hotel. The bus stopped at the light.

"Ladies and gentlemen," I announced, "on your right is the Hollywood La Brea Gateway, but we just call it 'the Four Ladies Statue.' It pays tribute to L.A.'s multi-ethnic history by honoring four great women of early Hollywood: Dolores del Rio, the Mexican star; Dorothy Dandridge, the first African-American woman to be nominated for an Academy Award in a leading role; Anna May Wong, the first Chinese-American star; and Mae West. Well, you know about Mae West! She..."

The bus started up again and turned the corner. The Gateway was behind us. Oh, no! I didn't get a chance to say anything about Mae West! Or the sculptor, Catherine Hardwicke! I didn't even mention the tiny statue of Marilyn Monroe on top of the gazebo! Whatever made me think I could be a tour guide?

The driver pulled up and stopped at the next light, and I could see that he was laughing. My humiliation was complete.

He leaned over, cupped his right hand against his cheek, and whispered, "I've been driving this bus for two years, and you're the first tour guide that ever remembered all four of their names."

I leaned across the aisle, cupped my left hand against my cheek, and whispered back, "It's my first tour."

He sat up straight and said, loudly, "This is your first tour? What the hell were you doing before, brain surgery?"

I learned three things that day:

1. Don't tell the driver it's your first tour. At least, not until it's all over and the passengers are out of earshot.

2. You can leave out a whole lot of things you meant to say, and nobody but you will ever know.

3. I might just be able to do this guiding stuff after all!

I decided to commit to proper training for the profession. My goal was to become an international tour director and to see the world while getting paid for it. I enrolled in America's premier travel school, the International Tour Management Institute (ITMI), founded in 1976 by Ted Bravos and the late Bill Newton. Bill and Ted (and Joanne Connors and Randy Hellrung) showed me what it meant to be a true travel-industry professional and opened up a marvelous world of experiences that have enriched my life immeasurably.

One of the most rewarding aspects of the job has been working with local guides all over the world. It's been an eye-opening education.

From Nonna, in Russia, I learned how to avoid catching cold after a long city tour on a frigid, rainy September day in St. Petersburg: "Take a hot shower the minute you get in; that's what *we* do."

From Malcolm, in South Africa, I learned how the queen of a gigantic termite mound knows which type of egg to lay: "The queen spends her entire life in a little cell deep in the mound. Workers of different types come to her and feed her. She can tell from their saliva how many workers of each kind are needed, so she lays that kind of egg – 30,000 eggs a day for twelve years."

And from Rakesh, our devout Hindu guide in India, came a single word that gave me one of the most moving insights into a culture I have ever experienced. One day, I asked him, "When you see a donkey being beaten, do you think, 'Oh, that poor donkey; I feel so sad,' or 'That must have been a wicked man in a former life; I'm glad he's being punished?'" Rakesh answered, simply, "Both."

When someone far from home gives you a kindly piece of survival advice, a fascinating bit of natural history, or a profound glimpse into an exotic culture, in that moment an ordinary trip is transformed into a journey of discovery and of human connection.

And a great guide, your cultural ambassador, has made all the difference.

Whether you are already a veteran tour guide or tour director, or if you are just entering this rewarding profession, I hope that this book will stimulate your creative juices and give you plenty of useful ideas for working with your colleagues and your clients – and a few laughs in the bargain.

If you're a traveler interested in what makes a guide truly special, or if you're an armchair traveler who enjoys reading stories from the road and is just along for the ride, you are most welcome, too. Happy Trails!

Joemy Wilson
Los Angeles, 2013

1

INTRODUCTION

———

What Makes a Tour Guide Great?

This book will describe, chapter by chapter, all the qualities that I believe make a great guide: Empathy, Common Sense, Adaptability, Flexibility, Knowledge, Technique, Personal Style, and Passionate Enthusiasm. To illustrate these qualities, I've used anecdotes from over two decades of travel on seven continents. We'll join city tours, walking tours, and multi-day tours, and we'll explore the unique challenges of these different travel scenarios. Through these stories from the road, you will see how a guide can make or break a traveler's experience. Serving as a cultural ambassador is an enormous responsibility!

Coming Up on Your Left is a how-to book, but it's also a how-not-to book. While traveling and working with guides all over the globe, I was astonished when I began to notice a pattern of common errors and bad habits that even the best guides tend to fall into, no matter where in the world they guide!

So I devised three simple rules to keep in mind that can help prevent these common, avoidable mistakes, and to stop thoughtless remarks before they are spoken. I share these little rules with you in this guidebook, along with the anecdotes and a few practical checklists.

But this is primarily a book of stories. After all, storytelling is what we guides do!

Whenever I've given an example of what *not* to say or do, I've omitted or changed the name of the guide in question. For their privacy, I have also changed the names of any passengers mentioned in the anecdotes.

To avoid either sexism or the awkward *he/she* construction, I will alternate between *she* and *he* when mentioning tour directors, drivers, and guides. Fortunately for us all, the travel industry is an Equal Opportunity Employer!

Are you ready for a trip around the world? Fasten your seat belt and let's hit the road!

2

EMPATHY

———

I Want a Leopard and I Want It Now

He reminded me of the young Denzel Washington, but he was even cuter. His smile was dazzling as he held out his hand and shook mine firmly. "I'm K.G. – like *kilogram*," he said.

That was my initial meeting with one of the best guides I've ever worked with. K.G.'s territory was the Sabi Sabi Private Game Reserve, a magnificent expanse of African bushveld in the southwestern section of South Africa's massive Kruger National Park. K.G. knew every mile of the bewildering tangle of dirt roads that meandered through the reserve, and he was intimate with the habits of all the animals in the park, from the famous Big Five – lion, leopard, elephant, rhino, and Cape buffalo – to the smaller mammals, birds, reptiles, and the tiniest insects.

K.G. was knowledgeable, charming, and full of passion for his work, like all the rangers I worked with during many years of leading South African safaris. What set him apart was the deep wisdom he showed one day, when one of my guests refused to go on the last evening game drive of our stay.

Allie was a world traveler and a bit world-weary at this point in her life. She was sick to death of safaris that failed to thrill her.

"I've been on safaris all over Africa, and I've never seen a leopard. I've always wanted to see one in the wild and it just hasn't happened. I never have any luck."

I said, "Well, we have one more chance tonight. You never know. This game drive could be the one!"

Allie said, "We didn't see a leopard yesterday and we didn't see one this morning. And this place is supposed to have lots of leopards. That's why I came."

Allie was right about that. The Sabi Sabi reserve boasts all the Big Five, but it's known for being especially rich in leopards, which are solitary, territorial animals, invariably described in travel brochures as "elusive." K.G. and his tracker had been following fresh tracks that morning on our earlier game drive, but the leopard remained its elusive self. I reminded Allie that there was definitely one in the area.

"Oh, why should I bother? It's nice here at the lodge. I'll just sit on the deck and read, and I'll see you at dinner when you get back."

As a tour director, I always try to maximize my guests' experience and encourage participation, wherever we are in the world. But at a certain point, I give up. If a guest insists on, say, doing crosswords in the back of the motor coach all through the Alps or sitting out a safari, eventually I admit that it's her vacation and she's entitled to enjoy it however she likes. So I left Allie in the lobby lounge and went out to meet the others.

I walked over to K.G.'s Land Rover. The other two in our group were already in it and raring to go.

"Where's Allie?" asked K.G. I told him she'd given up on ever seeing a leopard in her life.

"That's ridiculous! She has to come! I am definitely going to find a leopard tonight!"

"Well, I tried to convince her, but…"

K.G. said, "Wait here a minute; I'll go get her."

Three minutes later he was back, with Allie in tow. She still didn't look convinced, but K.G. had turned that mega-watt smile on her, told her he was not driving back to the lodge that night until he had found her a leopard, and simply refused to take no for an answer. She climbed into the Land Rover and we were off.

I'm sure you can guess what happened next. We hadn't been riding for ten minutes when suddenly, there it was – one of the most exquisite leopards I'd ever seen! She was right there on the road, striding purposefully ahead, ignoring us completely. We drove alongside her for a super-close look and a photo opportunity worthy of *National Geographic*.

I looked at Allie's face. I don't think I've ever seen a happier person in my life. Except maybe K.G., who looked proud to the point of bursting.

"She's hunting," said K.G. And so she was. In a few minutes, the big cat turned off the road and slunk into the bush.

We could still see her stalking through the grass. Suddenly, she pounced! We heard one quick *yip* and then silence. Our leopard had herself a mongoose.

"She would have preferred an impala, but this will do for a nice appetizer," said K.G., as he followed her off-road. She took her prize to a nice picnic spot under a tree, and we watched her enjoy her snack.

The next morning, when we left the park on our way to Johannesburg, I gave all the rangers and trackers their tip envelopes and thanked them for their usual terrific work. When I got to K.G., I gave him two envelopes. One was the official tour company one. The second was from me.

The note inside said: *Thank you for Allie's leopard. And thank you for being my teacher.*

But I Didn't Major in Psychology

You may wonder why I consider empathy such a critical quality for a tour guide to have, perhaps even the most important. Yes, K.G.'s ability to connect emotionally with Allie enabled him to use all his charm to give her a travel experience she'll never forget. But, you may think, surely that sort of thing doesn't come up very often? How frequently would a local guide have to persuade someone to participate in a wonderful activity that she's already paid for? Why should a guide have to be a psychologist, too?

True, the safari was an unusual situation. But empathy is necessary even in ordinary touring circumstances. Consider the following scenario. Put yourself in the place of an eager traveler who has come halfway around the world, at great expense and nursing a killer case of jet lag, to see the beauties of South Africa.

You are sitting on a deluxe motor coach in front of your lovely Cape Town hotel, excited and all ready for a full-day tour of the spectacular Cape Peninsula. You've read up about South Africa and have always wanted to see how people are living in the post-apartheid era, go on safari, and enjoy the magnificent scenery. It's a trip of a lifetime, and because of the distance and expense, these precious two weeks will almost certainly represent your only chance to visit the country.

Your tour director, after a few words of welcome and a couple of brief logistical announcements, introduces your local guide for the day and hands her the mike.

"Good morning, ladies and gentlemen," the guide says. "First we are going to drive through Cape Town for a quick orientation of the city before we head down to Cape Point. However, the route we usually would take, Chapman's Peak, is closed. It's the most beautiful part of the trip and one of the most scenic coastal drives in the world. I'm sorry I won't be able to show it to you today, but because of corruption in our government, they haven't cleared the rocks from landslides off the road to make it safe for traffic for several months now. So we'll be taking an alternate route."

Do you think I'm kidding, or exaggerating? No. I was the tour director on that trip, and I'm quoting as close to verbatim as my shocked brain was able to record. Was this a rookie, on her first assignment? No. She was a knowledgeable and experienced 20-year veteran.

If that guide had had any empathy for the people on her tour, not to mention an ounce of common sense, she would have realized that her words had just instantly transformed a bunch of excited, happy campers into a group of sad, disappointed – perhaps even angry – travelers. For most if not all of them, this was to be their only journey to South Africa. The country is thousands of miles from practically everywhere. It's an expensive luxury trip. Even for those with time and money to burn, there are so many other wonderful places in the world to see.

When we got to the morning rest stop, I pulled our guide aside and asked what in the world she'd been thinking. Why did she tell the travelers about a highlight that they weren't going to be lucky enough to see?

"Oh," she said, casually, "by the next time they come, the road will be fixed, and they can see it then."

Saddest of all, she had made what political pundits call an unforced error. It happens in electoral campaigns all the time. This is when a politician says something stupid, damaging, and totally unnecessary.

There was no mention of Chapman's Peak in the brochure or in any of the travel documents the guests had been given. There was no reason whatsoever for the guide to apologize for not seeing it. If, on the other hand, that particular routing *had* been in the brochure or the travelers' documents, the guests would have gotten notification and an explanation of the road closure from the tour company. That's their responsibility, not the local guide's job.

Of course, there's always the possibility that someone on the coach might raise his hand, waving a guidebook, and say, "Hey, I've just read that there's a beautiful coastal road here called Chapman's Peak. Why aren't we going that way?"

Then the guide can say something like, "Yes, that is a very pretty drive, but it's closed for safety reasons. We're going to be taking an equally beautiful route today. You'll see plenty of great coastal scenery, and it will be perfectly safe. And our route today is a bit shorter, so we'll be able to give you some extra time to explore Cape Point."

Spin? Sure. But a lie? No, not really. It *is* all gorgeous. (A tour director colleague of mine refers to South Africa as "California, except more so, with big animals.") Extra time at a spectacularly scenic destination? Always good. By pointing out these positive aspects of the situation, the guide could have shown that she really wanted her guests to have a great time.

Did you notice another unforced error my guide made? Nobody had brought up the issue of government corruption. It's a tricky subject to talk about anyway; why introduce it? Again, if someone should ask about current governmental policies, the guide could give a brief, balanced answer, inviting questions off the coach to those who might be interested in delving further into the local political situation.

Unforced errors such as these can be avoided when Empathy joins up with its most valuable partner: *Common Sense*.

3

COMMON SENSE

If Only You'd Been Here Last Week

Here's another example of what not to say, on a different continent. Put yourself in the position of this elderly guest:

You are on a motor coach, driving through magnificent Alpine scenery. It's a bit overcast, and rain is predicted for later in the day, but the clouds hovering over the mountaintops, slightly obscuring the peaks, lend the landscape a mystical, evocative atmosphere. Below the clouds you can see wide valleys of emerald green grass, carpeted with wildflowers and dotted with rustic chalets and contented cows. A river meanders through the valley. You're sitting in the front seat today and can hardly believe your good luck. It's a dream of a lifetime come true! You are finally seeing the Alps! It's just as lovely as you always thought it would be. You are drifting along in bliss, thinking, *Thank goodness I was able to manage it now. I'm getting too old to travel any more.*

The guide across the aisle from you turns to the tour director and says, off the mike but loudly enough for the first few rows to hear:

"Remember how beautiful it was last time? Not a cloud in the sky and all the snowy peaks against the blue? Too bad the visibility is so bad today!"

Are you in tears yet? It was hard for me not to cry. You guessed it; I was the tour director on the receiving end of that depressing and totally unnecessary weather report. And if you guessed that this was not a rookie, but a veteran national guide who otherwise did brilliant work, you guessed right again.

Empathy and Common Sense will help you to abide by my Rule #1 for local guides:

RULE #1:
THIS IS THE BEST OF ALL POSSIBLE TOURS!

Put yourself into the shoes of a visitor. Don't rave about gorgeous sights they can't see, or recommend fabulous activities they won't have time to do. Don't describe the most incredible local dish in your favorite restaurant that closed yesterday for remodeling. And don't tell them how perfect the weather was last week or how much more exciting the city is when you come in the summertime or how much better everything looks when it's not pouring down rain.

Ironically, the more experienced you are, the more likely you are to fall into this trap. As a veteran local guide, you have seen the same place in different ways so many times that memories and comparisons can't help but pop into your head. This is good. All that experience deepens your insights and can enrich your commentary. But you don't always have to say what you're thinking out loud!

Once in St. Petersburg, the first thing a local guide said to my group after I introduced her and handed her the mike was, "Unfortunately, White Nights are over." Do you think I ever requested *her* again?

What if a guest brings up the subject? If someone is unhappy about the weather, or thinks he might miss out on a special opportunity he's heard about, you can use a little bit of the old spin:

"White Nights are over? True, but how nice for you – it's so much less crowded! Plus you'll be able to get some sleep!"

"Yes, it is overcast today, but look how pretty the wildflowers are in the mist – aren't they colorful? Listen! Don't you love how mysterious the cowbells sound?"

"Yes, that restaurant used to be quite nice, but let me give you the address of a really special place near your hotel – and it's open tonight!"

You get the idea. If it's not possible *on that trip* for your clients to see it, do it, eat it, feel it, or otherwise experience it, *don't mention it*. Even if you know perfectly well that this is not the Best of All Possible Tours, do everything you can to let the guests believe it is. If you privately think it's a pity these poor folks have arrived out of season, find something wonderful about that season to brag about.

Here's an example. I have led tours of Victoria Falls from the Zimbabwe side in every month of the year except December. A travel agent may tell her clients that the optimum viewing period for this spectacular natural wonder is May through early August. But the great local guides I work with in Zim know that any time of the year a visitor comes to Vic Falls is absolutely the Best Possible Time to be there, and they will prove it.

In January through April, the falls are so high that you get drenched walking along them. *Exciting, isn't it?* my guides will ask. *Look at those rainbows!* In late August through October, half the gorges are bare and the basalt cliffs are showing. *Wow! An open geology book!* In November, the rains begin again. So does life! Everywhere amongst the lush tropical greenery are brilliant red fireballs and flame lilies, early Christmas decorations from Mother Nature. Tiny, adorably ugly newborn warthog piglets scurry after their mothers, their little tails like antennas straight up in the air. You would never see these marvels during the high season! *How smart you were to come now*, the Zim guides will tell you.

In all the tours of Victoria Falls I have led over the years, I never once heard a guest complain that he'd chosen the wrong season, thanks to my local guides and their enormous pride in their great national treasure.

If someone is really unhappy about the weather, the season, the itinerary, or anything else, just tell the tour director, so she can deal with it. Major spin is *her* job. My first mentor, tour director extraordinaire Mary Harold, was brilliant at this. Informed of a power outage, she turned to the group with a big smile and said, "Guess what! Tonight we're having a candlelight dinner!"

Let the tour director take care of problems. You, the guide, are the storyteller. Your job is to entertain, inform, and inspire. This leads us to Rule #2:

RULE #2:
SHOW-AND-TELL IS FOR GROWNUPS, TOO!

Imagine you are a passenger on a tour of Southeast Asian highlights in Vietnam, Cambodia, and Thailand. All your life you've dreamed of visiting the Angkor Archeological Park in Cambodia to see Angkor Wat, a magnificent 12th-century Khmer temple complex and the largest Hindu temple in the world. You will be there only a few hours. Naturally, you want to maximize your time and see as much as possible.

Your travel documents say you'll depart Ho Chi Minh City for Siem Reap on a late morning flight, check into the hotel, have lunch, and then head out for the temples. Your first stop in the park will be Angkor Wat. You can barely sleep the night before. You imagine the thrilling moment of your first view of those mystical towers rising above the jungle.

Except, of course, that things don't always work out as planned. Your tour director warned you that "late morning flight" could more properly be translated as "early afternoon flight" due to almost predictable airport delays at that time of year, and he was absolutely right. By the time you arrive at the hotel and set off again, you have only two precious hours before the park closes at 6:00 pm.

You are a seasoned traveler and know that these things happen. There's nothing to be done about a flight delay. You lean back and tell yourself to relax.

Finally you are almost there. Your anticipation is rising as the bus cruises along beside the moat that encloses the huge temple. You find yourself a bit annoyed that the local guide has been chatting with the driver part of the way, and when he does give commentary, he's been talking about anything and everything *except* the temples.

There it is! The bus stops, and you and the other passengers get out. The guide leads you to a spot across from Angkor Wat, not directly in front of the main entrance, but off to the side. You can't yet see the temple very well. You are all standing together under a tree, and the guide begins to explain the history of the complex.

Twenty minutes later, you are still standing there and the guide is still talking. He's given a full explanation of the history, the features, the architecture, and the symbolism of the temple as a microcosm of the Hindu universe. However, you weren't able to concentrate on a word he said, because you were so anxious to actually *visit* the temple! And you were so late getting there! Why would the guide want to add another delay?

Why? Because he forgot that *Show-and-Tell Is for Grownups, Too!* Everybody wanted to *see* the temple, not just hear about it. What could he have done instead, if he had felt empathy for his clients and used his common sense? You know the answer.

All he had to do was give the information about Angkor Wat on the bus, beginning about twenty minutes before we arrived there. (Yes, as you've probably already figured out, the eager, frustrated passenger in that scenario was yours truly.) Then we could have hopped out, walked along the moat to the entrance of the main causeway leading into the temple, paused for a moment of awed appreciation, taken a few photos, and walked straight in. Then our knowledgeable guide could *show* us all the interesting features of the temple and *tell* us about them at the same time!

I Didn't Come Here to Stand Under a Tree

I had a similar experience in Turkey a couple of years later. The group I was traveling with left Istanbul on an early morning flight to Izmir. After lunch, we were off for the archeological site of Sardis, capital of the ancient kingdom of Lydia.

Sardis has a gorgeous setting and a fascinating history, involving Persians, Greeks, Romans, Alexander the Great, Tamerlane, and innumerable other conquerors. It was once a great trading center. The local river ran with specks of gold dust from a nearby mountain. Coinage was invented there. Its last Lydian king, Croesus, was so wealthy that he gave us the phrase "as rich as Croesus." The site includes a partly restored bath and gymnasium complex, a synagogue, and a temple devoted to Artemis. These evocative ruins are all scattered around a sleepy little village in a valley ringed by craggy mountains.

Plenty of juicy commentary for the national guide to give us on the ninety-minute ride from Izmir to Sardis, right? Except he barely said a word. When we got there, he gathered us all under a tree, within sight of the gymnasium, and talked for ten minutes.

It was hot. We walked through the first site, which was quite impressive. Then we got back on the bus and rode a short distance over to the Temple of Artemis, on the other side of town. Did he introduce the Temple of Artemis on the way? What do you think?

We arrived at the site, and he said, "Oh, you must be so tired. Let's all sit down here; it's shady." He indicated some wide marble steps. The group sat – with their backs to the rest of the temple! – while he talked about it. Everyone, that is, but a few of us who were determined to actually see the site. We renegades spent the fifteen minutes of his lecture wandering and photographing the magnificent ruins and the spectacular mountain scenery. We got back to the rest of the group in time to hear him say, "OK, let's get on the bus now."

He didn't talk much on the way back to Izmir, either. He mostly just sat there, staring out the window, occasionally chatting with the driver. He perked up just before we got back to the hotel.

I asked him the next day why he hadn't given his commentary on the way out. He said, "Oh, I knew most of them were so tired they would just sleep through my commentary anyway."

Empathic? Obviously, he thought so. *Poor weary travelers, done in by a short flight and a big lunch! I'll be kind to them. I'll let them sleep, and when we get to the site I'll even let them stand in the shade! What a good, thoughtful guide I am!*

We were all healthy adults, ranging in age from twenty-five to about seventy. Why was he so sure we were too exhausted to hear a few remarks on the bus about a fascinating place we were about to visit? Why did he think it would be less tiring to stand under a tree for ten minutes instead, lengthening an already long travel day?

He may have thought it was his wonderful empathy for the group. I would call it professional laziness and lack of common sense.

Consider this: If he was so sure that most of his guests would simply sleep whether he spoke or not, why not give commentary to those who were keen to learn about his beautiful country and let the others sleep? I wasn't asleep, and I was not the only one. Sure, some of the folks nodded off. Can you say *Self-fulfilling Prophecy?*

Here is my wish list for that ninety-minute ride:

- *Give about fifteen minutes of general commentary on Izmir (the third-largest city in Turkey), its people, and how they live. Our route took us through a mixed urban, suburban, agricultural, and industrial area; flatlands, with mountains in the distance. It was not the most beautiful part of Turkey by any means, but not totally devoid of interest. I was intrigued by the amazingly large number of massive suburban high-rise developments up against the mountains in the distance. Did tens of thousands of people live way out there and commute into this valley to harvest crops and work in the quarries and cement plants? When did all this development happen?*
- *Play about half an hour of some traditional Turkish music at low volume, followed by about half an hour of silence.*
- *Now it's time for a gently humorous wake-up call. "Maybe you missed a few of those cement factories. That's OK. You can catch them on the way back. But now, the scenery is going to get really pretty, and wait until you see Sardis! It's an amazing place." Then introduce Sardis for about fifteen minutes, with plenty of enthusiasm!*

Forget standing under that tree. Get right into the site and visit that gymnasium!

On the way back, sure, let them sleep most of the way. But I'll bet at least some of those travelers would love to hear about you and your life in a country that's new and different to them. Wouldn't you like to become one of their favorite travel memories?

Another guide in Turkey handled a similar archeological excursion beautifully. A couple of days after Sardis, we visited Perge, an extensive Greco-Roman complex about an hour outside of Antalya. Perge is another cultural hybrid that was also once under Lydian and Persian rule and had been conquered by the inevitable Alexander the Great. We heard about this history on the way there, and we were told about various artifacts discovered in Perge that we would see later at the Antalya Museum.

Just outside the entrance, we drove past the ancient theater and stadium. Since these impressive ruins were closed for renovation, our guide did not point them out or even mention them. Remember Rule #1, *This Is the Best of All Possible Tours?* He did.

When we arrived at Perge, we entered through the Roman gate and spent the next forty-five minutes walking with our guide. We saw the Roman walls, a ruined basilica, the agora, and the mighty circular towers of the Hellenistic gate.

It was hot. Very, very hot. Our guide led us into the Roman baths and suggested we sit down in the shade so he could tell us about them. What a great idea! In the shadow of the ancient walls of the baths, we sat where the Romans used to sit and listened with interest to the description of frigidarium, tepidarium, and caldarium as they were pointed out to us, while gratefully drinking our own frigid water from the chilled bottles so thoughtfully provided.

Refreshed after a fifteen-minute talk and a lively Q&A session, we went on to the colonnaded street, where our guide pointed out the old Roman water channel, the remains of ancient shops, and the nymphaeum. From there, it is possible to take a rough little hike to an acropolis hill for a panoramic view, but since we had no time for this, our guide didn't mention it, once again letting Rule #1 be *his* guide. We spent a little free time on our own and slowly made our way back to the entrance.

Naturally, you're not always going to have an ideal situation. Suppose you're meeting your clients at the site and don't have any time on the bus? Suppose there's a line and you can't get in right away? Suppose there's no place to sit? Then you do the best you can. But whenever it's possible, here's my idea of a model plan when making a major site visit:

- *Give your introduction on the coach.*
- *Get out. Walk, stop, show and tell. Repeat.*
- *Optional: Let them sit in a comfortable and pretty spot while you show and tell some more. Get up and walk. Show and tell again.*
- *Give them free time, if appropriate.*
- *Walk back and board the coach. Ask if there are any questions.*

I Can't Hear You; My Legs Are Tired

Incidentally, I think guides sometimes don't realize how fatiguing it can be to stand still for a long time, especially for seniors. It's much easier to walk around slowly, pause a moment or two, and then continue. It's more engaging, too, particularly in a setting that's extensive and rich in visual interest. When one moves about, enabling the scenery or cityscape to shift, the perception is refreshed and the ear becomes more receptive to commentary.

The longest I can ever recall having to stand in one spot on a tour was in Havana, Cuba, at the Casa de Africa. It's a small but interesting museum, with exhibits ranging from *Santería* to slavery, and some excellent modern artwork.

Our local guide took us to the museum and introduced our small group to the docent. They led us upstairs to a display of *orishas*, deities whose function for *santeros* (believers in *Santería*) is similar to that of Catholic saints or the ancient Greek gods. The *orishas* were arranged in a corner of a large room with many other displays.

The walls in that corner were draped in large swags of red, blue, white, and yellow cloth. In front of the drapes were several stands, covered in more cloths of the same colors, as well as green, purple, and pink. On top of these display platforms were doll-sized representations of Cuba's favorite *orishas*, among some four hundred of these deities: Chango, king of the gods, garbed in red; Yemayá, mother of the gods, in blue; Ochun, whose bright yellow dress stood for love and sensuality; and Obatalá, in white, for peace.

Our docent was knowledgeable. She spoke with enthusiasm about the fascinating Afro-Cuban syncretistic religion, a holdover from the era of slavery but with deep spiritual significance for millions of contemporary Cubans. Just standing there in front of the small, wildly colorful display was a powerful cultural experience. For a few minutes, that is. Then we were ready to move on to the rest of the room and the other parts of the museum. There was plenty more to see.

We did not move on, however. The docent continued speaking and, since she spoke only Spanish, the local guide had to translate everything she said into English. This, of course, doubled the length of her talk.

Have you ever tried to stand in one spot without moving, listening to a lecture, for half an hour? It is not easy. Our feet and legs and hips and backs were beginning to complain, silently but insistently.

I hated to appear rude, but halfway through the docent's presentation, I began gradually edging away from our group, walking up to the displays of other sacred objects – masks, musical instruments, and symbolic drawings on the walls. I snapped some photos. Then I glanced out the open window at the beautifully restored building across the street, newly painted in blue and yellow.

Suddenly, a young man in a red shirt and blue pants, proud and handsome as Chango himself, stepped out onto the wrought-iron balcony. The colors in my viewfinder replicated the colors of the display behind me. I took a few quick photos of this *orisha* come to life.

Cuba must be one of the hardest places in the world just to stand in one spot for a long time. Practically anywhere you turn, something magical appears! Cuba makes you want to keep turning, keep moving, keep seeing more.

Behind me, the others shifted from one foot to another and began to drift about the room, too. The docent kept talking, and our guide kept on dutifully translating. Finally, they led us downstairs, past a large exhibit on slavery in Cuba and into the courtyard, where we were treated to a dramatic dance performance with a live conga band.

It was a fascinating visit. But it would have been even better if we had been able to see the exhibit on slavery, such an important part of Cuba's history, and gotten some information on the mysterious-looking sacred objects in the other rooms we glimpsed. And our feet (and legs and hips and backs) would have been happier, too.

Most docents are especially knowledgeable and have a deep emotional attachment to their work, and generally they want to share as much as possible. Unfortunately, they don't often have the opportunity to do an introduction in advance because they usually meet their guests at the site.

If you're a guide who works regularly with a docent who has a tendency to spend the entire visit stuck in one little corner, you can help. Gently suggest that you would like to give a basic introduction on the way to the site, and that she can then cover more rooms or exhibits. She might wish to give the visitors a little time to explore the site on their own, if that is permitted.

For instance, here's how our Cuban guide could have played the hero. She could have rescued us in advance by providing a lively, brief chat in the van as we rode from the hotel to the museum, outlining the basic beliefs of *Santería* and its development in Cuba. She could have introduced us to the major *orishas* by name and told us of the personalities, attributes, and colors associated with each one.

Upon arrival at the museum, she could have told the docent, "These visitors know a little about *Santería*, and they are so eager to hear more from you. First, let's see how many of the *orishas* they can identify when they see your beautiful display upstairs!"

As a traveler, wouldn't you have felt delighted, and so clever, if you could have picked out Chango, and maybe one or two of the others, from that corner display? Wouldn't you then have felt more engaged, more involved, more invested in what the docent had to say?

Another benefit of a pre-visit orientation is that now there is time to see more of the museum, especially in a case like this where translation is involved. You don't need a degree in higher mathematics to figure out that a ten-minute introductory talk in the van just bought your clients an extra twenty minutes to experience Casa de Africa, right?

And you don't need a degree in psychology to have empathy and use your common sense to adapt to the needs of your guests. Probably you are already a very nice person, full of care and concern for others. Otherwise, why would you have gone into the field of travel, a service business that's devoted to sharing sights and insights?

The empathy is surely there within you. I'm sure you have plenty of common sense. Whenever you meet a new group, just ask yourself: *How can I make this one of the most memorable visits of their lives?* Rule #2 can help. *Show-and-Tell Is for Grownups, Too!*

Give the introduction in advance, preferably on the coach, if there is one. If not, give it at the hotel or other pickup point if at all possible, or even in a short handout. Walk into the site – cathedral, temple, museum, park, whatever – upon arrival.

Of course, some attractions and sites have lines and you can't enter right away. If you're guiding at the Hermitage, or the Blue Mosque, or Nefertari's Tomb, you're at the mercy of the gatekeepers and you probably won't get in the minute you arrive. If you are guiding just a few people and can brief them while waiting, great. But if it's a larger group, do give the introduction beforehand and get in as quickly as the line allows you to.

If there is no time with the group in advance and no opportunity to sit in a spot that's both comfortable and visually interesting before or during the tour, and you absolutely have to huddle in a corner somewhere after entering to introduce the site, make as brief a speech as possible and get moving as soon as you can.

Show this wonderful place to your guests, and tell them more about it while they are walking around, seeing it through their eyes and yours. They will love you for it, and they will think you are the best guide in the world.

Next we will explore two more important qualities for guides, *Adaptability* and *Flexibility.* Like Empathy and Common Sense, they work together.

4

ADAPTABILITY AND FLEXIBILITY

―――

Know Your Audience, Flow with Your Audience

It was a dream assignment. Marilyn and I were chosen to lead a small-ship cruise tour of Japan and South Korea. Neither of us had been to Japan before, so the tour company sent us ahead for training. On the cruise portion, we were to train ourselves by keeping eyes and ears open and exploring as much as possible. But in Tokyo and Kyoto, the cities at the beginning and end of the cruise, we were assigned one of the best guides in each city, who had been told to show us everything they could cram into a few days.

Marilyn and I arrived in Tokyo in the late afternoon. My flight had been fourteen hours; hers, seventeen. Neither of us had slept. We were too excited to sleep, too busy studying our guidebooks and trying to memorize Polite Japanese Phrases. We were also too revved up with adrenaline to notice any jet lag as we got off the plane.

Our guide, the young and lovely Matsuda-san, brought us to the hotel to check in and freshen up. She then asked if she could take us to dinner at "a traditional Japanese place." We said by all means; please take us somewhere that you would go yourself.

The restaurant was below street level, small, dark, crowded, and hip. It was a sushi bar, full of fashionable young women and intense salarymen. The specialty was chicken sashimi.

Marilyn and I were in Tokyo for the first time in our lives, literally rubbing shoulders with the locals and eating slices of raw chicken heart. (It was delicious, and yes, it tasted like...chicken.) We were in heaven, experiencing the *real* Tokyo with Matsuda-san and hearing about all the tourist attractions she planned to show us in the next couple of days – the Tokyo Tower, the Imperial Palace gardens, the Asakusa Temple, Shinjuku, Ginza, the Tsukiji fish market, the National Museum, more gardens, more temples, more museums....

Jet lag, food, and beer began to take their toll. Matsuda-san noticed our eyelids starting to close and our heads beginning to loll. She looked at us in dismay, as if we were a couple of kittens in a basket someone had left on her doorstep that she had no idea what to do with.

"What shall we do now?" she asked. "You are too old for nightclub, yes?"

Marilyn and I looked at each other. We looked back at Matsuda-san. In perfect unison we replied, "We are too old for nightclub, yes."

Could she have been a tiny bit more tactful? Sure. But she certainly knew her audience.

Getting to Know You

How do you get to know your audience? Usually whoever has hired you will give you your first clue. Then you start asking questions. The better you know your clients, the more you will be able to empathize with them and use your common sense to *adapt* to their needs and interests and to be *flexible* with your program.

Matsuda-san received specific instructions from her agency, our ground operator in Japan. She knew that she was getting two professional tour directors who had been instructed to learn as much about Tokyo as possible in a short time. The agency gave her the authority to organize our sightseeing efficiently, along with the necessary expense money for taxis, subway, admissions, and meals.

As Matsuda-san got to know us, her guiding experience and empathy with us led her to fill in the blanks: *They aren't young, but they seem adventurous. They've traveled a lot. And they're walking pretty fast for their age. No complaints about the crowded subway. Let's see – I'll take them to a great authentic, non-touristy restaurant, get them back to the hotel for a good night's sleep, and then show them twelve hours of tourist sights tomorrow.*

It didn't take our guide very long to realize that we were eager, energetic, and capable of covering a lot of ground, even if too old for nightclub.

Failure Is Such a Great Learning Experience

I learned an important lesson in knowing one's audience early in my career, during my first year of local guiding in Los Angeles. Shortly after that terrifying first tour described in the Preface, I was hired to lead a series of architectural tours and museum visits. As these assignments aligned perfectly with my own interests, they were a pleasure. Once I led a group of Belgian architects on a downtown walking tour to see the elegant Art Deco fixtures in the Oviatt Building and the Bradbury's magnificent filigree ironwork and glazed brick. Several times, I escorted art patrons to the Getty Museum, gave talks about architect Richard Meier and the construction of the campus, and helped my guests find the most interesting fossils in the travertine walls and walkways before sending them in to see the paintings. I became accustomed to pointing out lots of detail to very sophisticated audiences.

However, these delightful little specialty tours didn't come my way often enough to pay the mortgage, so I sent out more resumes.

I got my first student tour. I was the guide on Bus #16 out of eighteen. According to my documents, the group was "high-school students from New York of the Reform Jewish faith" here primarily to visit the Skirball Museum, an institution "dedicated to the American Jewish experience, using culture to bring people of all backgrounds together." Before the Skirball visit, each group would have a city tour, including Grauman's Chinese Theatre and the Hollywood Bowl.

I have limited experience with teenagers and had no idea how to engage them. The Belgian architects paid attention to me. The art patrons I took to the Getty hung on my every word. These kids? I might as well not have been there. They wanted to talk. They wanted to eat. I foolishly persisted in pointing out famous buildings and pretty architectural details, which were of no interest to these kids whatsoever. They enjoyed visiting the Chinese Theatre and the Hollywood Bowl, but they didn't seem interested in anything I had to say on the coach.

On the way to the Skirball, I noticed a big change. For ten minutes, the previously rowdy bunch listened attentively to my description of the cultural center, one of L.A.'s leading museums and among the most comprehensive Jewish cultural institutions in the world. It was as if they'd suddenly become a different group.

In hindsight, what I should have done is simple: ask the teacher what was important to the kids before starting the tour. She knew how interested in their cultural heritage her students were. I didn't even find out until after we got to the Skirball that they had just come back from Israel. If I had only taken a moment to chat with her first, I could have said something like this:

OK, everybody, listen up. I've got two questions for you. One: What is the Hollywood Bowl? And Two: Why is it important in Jewish history?

As I later discovered, they couldn't have answered either of those questions. But I would have gotten their attention and they would have listened if I had told them:

It's a huge open-air amphitheater in Hollywood where famous musicians from all over the world have performed – rock, jazz, classical, everything.

Did you know that lots of great Jewish artists who escaped the Nazis ended up in Los Angeles in the 1930s and 1940s? Many of them found work in Hollywood. Architects built movie sets, writers wrote scripts, and composers wrote film scores. These exiled artists became close friends, and on summer evenings, they all hung out at the Hollywood Bowl. Many legendary Jewish musicians performed there. Have you heard of the violinist Jascha Heifetz and the pianist Arthur Rubenstein? They played at the Bowl. Some of the refugees themselves appeared, such as the conductor Otto Klemperer. The Bowl became a gathering place for the émigré artists – kind of like a club you might have at school.

How I wish I could have those kids back again for a do-over! But it's too late. Most of them probably have kids of their own by this time. Whenever I'm in Hollywood, I still think about that day fourteen years ago and wish I could have gotten to know that audience sooner.

My only excuse is that I was still a beginner. I considered myself lucky just to *find* Bus #16 and felt grateful that I didn't lose half the group somewhere in Hollywood. At that early stage in my career, I was severely lacking in Adaptability and Flexibility. Fortunately, people continued to hire me, so I got the opportunity to learn from my mistakes and clean up my act.

As a free-lance guide in Southern California for several local companies, I often got notes about the group in advance. Memos on city-tour documents ranged from, say, "mature adults usually very interested in the narration" to "corporate wives who enjoy high-end shopping" and "high-school students from Japan who know a little English, with their teacher." These documents helped me to plan my approach with each group. The following three examples will show why it's necessary to adapt your approach beforehand and to remain flexible throughout a tour.

I planned to give the "mature adults" a comprehensive commentary. I find the early history of Los Angeles fascinating, so they heard plenty about the forty-four original settlers from Mexico and Spanish land grants. Imagine my surprise when I noticed that some of these folks "usually very interested in the narration" were chatting amongst themselves and ignoring me completely.

What they did love, however, was the movies. As soon as I introduced our upcoming stop at Grauman's Chinese Theatre on the Hollywood Walk of Fame, home to the world-famous Forecourt of the Stars, the chatting stopped. I had everyone's full attention as I described the handprints and footprints they would see there, of celebrities they grew up with, such as Marilyn Monroe, Humphrey Bogart, Elizabeth Taylor, George Burns, and Bob Hope. As far as they were concerned, mid-century film stars *were* Los Angeles history. Fortunately I picked up on this and kept to a movie-oriented theme for the rest of the tour.

The "corporate wives" turned out to be nine very sophisticated, well-traveled women who were just as interested in architecture as they were in buying luxury goods. When I dropped them off for their shopping spree in Beverly Hills, after giving them a map of Rodeo Drive showing all the upscale emporiums, one of them asked, "Where did you say the Frank Lloyd Wright building on Rodeo was? Please show me on the map." She and her friends headed there first.

The students from Japan who "knew a little English" turned out to understand as much English as I did Japanese, which is none. Fortunately, their teacher spoke excellent English. Also fortunately, she and I became friends instantly. We sat up front in the coach together. I pointed out landmarks and talked about the hottest rock stars and movie and TV personalities (*not* George Burns and Bob Hope, naturally), and she translated. While the kids explored Universal Studios, their teacher and I sat and had tea and talked and laughed for hours. She wanted to improve her practically perfect English, so I taught her some popular idioms of the day, such as *being on the same page* and *working 24/7*. She taught me *hello, goodbye, please,* and *thank you* in Japanese. I think we had at least as much fun as the students did.

With each new assignment I learned more about my craft. Paying careful attention to any clues I received in advance and to reactions during the tour gradually enabled me to establish better rapport with my clients, to adapt, and to be flexible. My lessons?

- Read the documents. But don't believe everything you read.
- If there's a group leader, ask her about the group's main interests and keep tuned in to their reactions.
- There is no such thing as a "general audience." Every group is unique.

An Almost Perfect Guide

I once led an American Heritage tour. We flew to Washington, D.C., and then continued to Mt. Vernon, Fredericksburg, Jamestown, Richmond, Monticello, Harpers Ferry, Gettysburg, Valley Forge, Amish Country, and Philadelphia. I probably got the assignment because I had once lived in Philadelphia and Washington. I took it because of the chance to see all those places I'd always wanted to visit but somehow missed when I lived back East, and get paid for it!

Local guides were assigned in Washington and Philly, but I was expected to give most of the other commentary. Even for a history buff, it was a lot of material to learn in a short time. Reading over the extensive day-by-day escort notes provided by the tour company, I was relieved to see that at least in Gettysburg, "Your local guide will provide all the in-depth commentary on the history and color surrounding this historic conflict."

He certainly did. Gary was great, one of the best guides at a historic site that I've ever heard. He made just one tiny error. Can you spot it? See if you can guess why I initially rated him just A rather than A plus.

Gary was a Licensed Battlefield Guide and really knew his stuff. His guiding technique was superb. He was adaptable and flexible. When we arrived, he took a moment to find out what I'd already told them about Gettysburg and geared his commentary accordingly. He asked me how much time they had. It was not nearly enough, but he managed to cram the official four stops on our itinerary into an hour and a half. "Sure wish you had a couple more hours," he said to me, privately.

The group was from all over the United States, mostly older couples, salt-of-the-earth types. Gary was friendly and engaging, establishing rapport and getting to know them right away. "Just call me Gary. Where are you folks from? Any of you gentlemen military veterans?" He interacted with the group throughout the tour and engaged them by both asking and answering questions.

Through Gary's stirring words, we were transported back to 1863. When he described Pickett's Charge, I could almost hear the artillery barrage and see Lee's army staggering away from Cemetery Hill in retreat. When he gave us Lincoln's Gettysburg address, from memory and full of expression, right on the spot where Lincoln himself had delivered it, many in the group were moved to tears. The visit was a profound, powerful experience, due to Gary's passionate enthusiasm for American history and the unique personal voice he had developed that enabled him to bring the Civil War to life right in front of our eyes.

Did you catch his tiny mistake? Here's a hint, if you need one: It's in the part where he was Getting to Know His Audience.

That's right. Gary asked, "Any of you gentlemen military veterans?" I quickly said, "Yes, many of the men, and two of the women have served as well." He recovered right away and thanked all the veterans on board for their service. As we walked through the battlefield, he even made a point of strolling alongside the two former WACs for several minutes, listening intently as they told him about their experiences in World War II.

Come to think of it, nobody's perfect. I think he deserves an A plus after all, don't you?

Gary had plenty of empathy and common sense. He adapted very quickly to the tiny mistake he made and more than made up for it. He was flexible with his timing. He also excelled in the next two areas we will look at, *Knowledge* and *Technique.*

5

KNOWLEDGE, AND A KEEN DESIRE TO KEEP ON LEARNING FOREVER

It's easy to do research these days. Just Google, right?

When I began guiding in 1998, Google was in its infancy and we were all still smarter than our phones. It took much longer in those days than it does now to put together commentary for a city tour, a site visit, or a multi-day tour across country.

I've already shared with you the terrors of my first Los Angeles city tour. That was mild compared to the fear that gripped me on another assignment a few months later.

I had taken several days of tour-guide training in San Diego, led by the lovely and energetic Cherie Anderson, who runs Professional Tour Management Training. Cherie is a former tour director and a superb trainer, and she gave us tons of great information on San Diego. The city is a natural for tourism, full of history and charm. The class strolled through the Gaslamp Quarter and Seaport Village, noting all the best restaurants for prospective guests. We marveled at the wealth of museums in Balboa Park and visited the legendary Hotel del Coronado, a National Historic Landmark. We got to know San Diego's fascinating Old Town, the first permanent Spanish settlement of Alta California – the Jamestown of the West Coast. I even earned a certificate that said I was a bona-fide San Diego guide. And so I was. Cherie had taught me well and I was full of knowledge and fired up with enthusiasm for my first assignment.

I drove down to San Diego and checked into the hotel, then spent the evening reviewing my commentary and the comprehensive escort notes provided by the tour company. In the morning, nattily dressed in the required navy-blue slacks and white polo shirt, I greeted my guests and we were off on the motor coach. Quickly I glanced at the paperwork to remind myself of the itinerary: through the Gaslamp Quarter, past the Del (*no stop, but tell them they can visit later*, said my helpful docs), through Balboa Park, and into Old Town for free time and lunch on their own. No problem! I know all those places. I'm a real San Diego guide!

Then I happened to notice a line at the bottom of the escort notes that I'd somehow missed. It said, "If asked, you are *from* San Diego."

Terror struck at my heart. How would I ever be able to convince anybody of that? I'm an Angeleno! I might as well have flown in from Duluth for all I really knew about San Diego.

I didn't know the name of the main newspaper. I didn't know what the football team was called. What if somebody asked me?

Today, of course, no problem. I'd just whip out the smartphone and surreptitiously Google. In 1998, that was not an option. My cellphone was the size of a brick, almost as heavy and just about as useful. I spent the entire morning in a flop sweat, meanwhile pointing out San Diego attractions nonstop. When we got to Old Town, I gave the group a little walking tour and then asked if there were any questions before I let them go for their free time, fingers crossed that nobody would ask me some basic fact I didn't know about my supposed home town.

Nobody did, of course. All they wanted to know was where to get a good margarita and a nice taco salad. That, I knew. Actually, in San Diego, it's hard to come up with a wrong answer to that question.

During my own free time, I found out the name of the paper and the football team (the Union-Tribune and the Chargers, in case you've been wondering), and sat down to enjoy a taco salad (hold the margarita until tonight, please). Halfway through lunch I started laughing at myself. It suddenly occurred to me how silly I'd been. I don't know everything about Los Angeles, either! Nobody was going to shoot me, or even fire me, if I had to say, "Good question! I don't know, but I'll find out for you." I was fine. The tour was fine. The sun was shining on beautiful San Diego and everybody was having fun.

If You're Gonna Rob the Stagecoach, Don't Ride Your Own Horse

They say a little knowledge is a dangerous thing. That may be, but a guide does need to have at least a *little* knowledge. A few years ago, while leading a series of tours in South Africa, I worked with a local guide who had practically none.

The itinerary took us on a flight from Cape Town to Mpumalanga, which means "the place where the sun rises" in Swazi. The province is such a scenic wonderland that the main road has been dubbed the Panorama Route. Funky little towns such as Graskop and Pilgrim's Rest are full of gold-rush lore.

Researching the history of Pilgrim's Rest was especially fun. It was declared a National Monument in 1986 and today its corrugated iron and timber buildings are preserved as a living history museum. Gold was discovered there in 1873 by a lone prospector, Wheelbarrow Patterson, who naturally tried to keep it a secret. Unfortunately for him, within three months after someone spotted old Wheelbarrow with a pan full of gold, he was joined at Pilgrim's Creek by fifteen hundred diggers frantically working their claims.

Stories from Pilgrim's Rest could easily have come from California in the days of the Forty-Niners. Claim jumpers were shot on sight, but for lesser offenses they just shaved off half your beard and drove you out of town. Lovely touch, that half beard, don't you think? Less painful than branding, but so humiliating!

Medicine was even more primitive than justice. There were few if any real doctors. One night, a drunken miner who was nursing a sick friend drank all of his patient's medicine by mistake but dutifully gave a spoonful of his own brandy every hour to his friend. (Both of them felt much better in the morning.)

The best part of the trip was the approach to Pilgrim's Rest over the road known as Robbers' Pass, because then I could tell the story of my favorite local character, the loveably inept Tommy Dennison. In 1899, two armed, masked men robbed a stagecoach just outside of town and got away with a fortune in gold. They were never caught. Thirteen years later, Tommy, a local barber, found himself in debt. He was such a popular fellow that everyone in town had lent him money, but he was unable to pay them back. Desperate, he decided to rob the stagecoach at the same spot on the mountain pass that had previously proved so successful.

Unfortunately, Tommy was as bad at planning as he was at handling money. The stagecoach he picked carried no gold, so all he got for his trouble was a few silver coins. He even rode his own horse for the robbery, so he was immediately recognized. When he got back into town, he tried to pay off his debts with the stolen money. Naturally, he was caught right away and thrown into jail. He served a five-year term.

When Tommy got out, he returned to Pilgrim's Rest, where he was astonished by the folk-hero's welcome he received. Everybody thought the sentence was far too harsh. They not only forgave him the debts he had tried so hard to repay but gave him more money to start a new business. Tommy then opened the Highwayman's Garage, which still stands today.

The first few times I ran the tour, I gave the commentary. Then the laws were changed. Foreign tour directors would no longer be allowed to do this; rather, they would be provided with a local guide in Mpumalanga. This was fine with me. As long as I still had my own job as tour director, I didn't care who told the stories. In fact, I looked forward to working with these guides and learning more about South Africa by listening to them.

Each time a different guide showed up. The first one was great. She was followed by another who was not bad. The next one was a different story. He was extremely young and had a very sweet smile but had obviously been given no training whatsoever. He just sat there silently, for miles. Occasionally he would say something like, "There's a bank." He mentioned a big waterfall you could go swimming in that was "down that road there." When we passed the Highwayman's Garage, he said, "There's a garage." I thought for sure he'd at least mention Tommy and gave him an expectant glance. He added, "You can get your car fixed there."

Since everyone on the bus had left his car in its very own garage at least 6,000 miles away, this was not terribly useful information. And although this was probably my guide's first assignment, when he mentioned a waterfall that nobody could see, let alone swim in, he managed to break Rule #1, *This Is the Best of All Possible Tours*, usually broken by Veteran Guides Who Know Too Much and Can't Keep It to

Themselves. I gently took the mike away, told him to sit back and relax, and gave the rest of the tour myself.

When I dropped off my guide, I gave him his tip envelope. Why not? He had shown up, ready and willing if not able, and put in the time. It wasn't his fault that the powers that be had thrown him to the wolves with no training.

Then I gave him a better tip. Pulling out my Mpumalanga commentary notes, I stuffed them into his hand and said, "Study these for next time."

After that, my tour company changed the routing and we didn't visit Pilgrim's Rest any more. So unfortunately I never saw my young friend again. However, I like to imagine him on his next tour and many tours thereafter, smiling his sweet smile and saying, "Ladies and gentlemen, coming up on your left is the Highwayman's Garage. That reminds me of a little story…."

One of the most knowledgeable guides I ever met was actually a former guide then working as our ground operator in Moscow. Natalia hired the guides and lecturers for incoming groups. Our Moscow program included a lecture on Russian history from a "Kremlin insider" whom Natalia booked for us.

One day, the lecturer called her to cancel at the last minute. No other speaker was available for my group at such short notice. Natalia showed up at the hotel herself and apologetically said that if it were OK with me, she would chat with the group instead. She's a beautiful and charming woman, and I knew my guests would enjoy her even if she read aloud for a while from the Moscow phone directory, so I said fine.

Natalia then proceeded to give the best *Russia Then and Now* talk that I had ever heard in that room. It was much livelier than the speech given by either of the official lecturers. She took questions from the group about corruption and current scandals, such as the Yukos/Khodorkovsky controversy that was then in the news, and her answers were much more forthcoming than any I had ever heard from either of the politicos.

Years later, I'm still amazed by that performance. Could you, at a moment's notice and without notes, give a sparkling, flawlessly organized forty-five minute talk on the history of your country and then tactfully and knowledgeably respond to a barrage of semi-hostile questions about the worst failings of your own government from a bunch of foreigners? Oh, and by the way, in your second language? No, me neither.

The Hardest Thing to See

If a little knowledge is a dangerous thing, what about a lot? Is it ever possible to have too much knowledge? Probably not, but it's possible to misuse it. We've already seen that a guide who has been over the same route many times is susceptible to making unfavorable comparisons with previous trips, when the weather was better or that great scenic road was open.

Another trap for experienced guides, especially if they have lived all their lives in the city or country where they are working, is that they know the place so well that they don't think to mention the obvious, which may be anything but obvious to the first-time visitor. The great German writer Johann

Wolfgang von Goethe summed it up perfectly (in German, of course). A somewhat abbreviated English translation is a popular entry in collections of wise quotes: *The hardest thing to see is what is in front of your eyes.*

An experience I had with a guide I've worked with for years in Austria is a great example of this common pitfall. Anneliese is one of the most knowledgeable guides I know, tops in her profession. Her lively and informative walking tour of Salzburg is a delight.

One day, we were running a new tour together in the countryside. Her commentary on the landscape, architecture, and history of the area was excellent as always. However, I didn't think the guests were paying her the attention she deserved. They seemed to be whispering amongst themselves. I tried to tune in to what they were saying but couldn't quite hear. So at the rest stop I asked a few people what was on their minds.

"We keep seeing these signs that say *Zimmer* or *Zimmer frei*. There's one on almost every house. What is this *Zimmer?*"

I told Anneliese. She was amazed. The signs were such a common sight to her, so ordinary, that it never occurred to her to mention them. Of course, the minute we were back on the coach, she cleared up the mystery for my American guests.

"In German, *Zimmer* means room, or rooms. People love to come out here to the mountains to stay for a few days to go hiking or skiing, depending on the season," she said.

That led to another mystery for one of the guests, who knew a little German. "Doesn't *frei* mean free? The rooms are free?"

Anneliese chuckled. "No, it doesn't mean the room is free of cost, it just means it's available! *Zimmer frei* means the same as a Vacancy sign in the United States. But the cost is reasonable. It's a popular way for townspeople to take a vacation, and it's a source of extra income for the farmers."

Being a great guide as well as a knowledgeable historian, Anneliese was flexible enough to add *Zimmer* to her repertoire for Americans and to share information about people's daily lives in Austria today as well as in centuries past. But I once had a guide in New York City who was stuck so firmly in the early 20th century that he literally forgot to notice the buildings around him.

The House of Mirth Is Right Around the Corner

He was advertised as one of the best guides in Manhattan. And he certainly was knowledgeable. However, he was so in love with Edith Wharton and the Old New York that she evoked so well in her writing that he seemed to notice only the sights that related to her novels, her life, or her contemporaries. As the coach drove slowly past Lincoln Center, one of the great performing arts centers of the world, home of the Metropolitan Opera and the New York Philharmonic, our guide was looking in the other direction and talking about *The Age of Innocence*. He never even pointed out the famous plaza fountain, the Met, or Avery Fisher Hall! It was as if Lincoln Center had never been built.

Now, I adore Edith Wharton myself, and this guide could have run a fine specialty tour – for the Edith Wharton Society. However, the group he had that day was expecting a standard New York City tour. Lincoln Center is a world-renowned highlight. Ignoring it is like giving a London tour and neglecting to point out Big Ben or guiding folks around Paris without a word about the Eiffel Tower.

Knowledge Is the Wing Wherewith We Fly to Heaven (William Shakespeare)

How do you get knowledge? From your own past experience, research on or off line, a tour training course, another guide, your driver, the tour company that hires you – sources of knowledge are practically endless.

If the person or company who hires you gives you a script or set of commentary notes, be sure to check it carefully. Back in my early Los Angeles tour guiding days, I worked for at least a dozen companies. Several of them sent me notes along with suggested routings. Here are just a few of the errors I found in various scripts:

- The wrong architect was credited with Hollywood's famed Capitol Records building. It was Louis Naidorf, not Welton Becket. Naidorf was working for Welton Becket Associates at the time, but Naidorf was the sole designer of the now iconic cylindrical tower.

- Credit for a Lloyd Wright residence was instead given to his father, Frank Lloyd Wright.
- A sculpture and fountain by Jacques Lipchitz at the Music Center was listed as *Dove of Peace.* The correct title is *Peace on Earth.* (The sculpture has a dove in it, but the title doesn't.)
- The oldest building in Los Angeles still standing, the Avila Adobe (c. 1818), was described as "still in use today as a restaurant." It is not; it's a museum.
- A classic Joni Mitchell song lamenting urban development in Los Angeles was referenced with severely mangled lyrics. I can't quote them here with the correct version without paying a royalty, but trust me – they were wrong!

Pedantic? Too picky? I don't know about you, but I make enough mistakes of my own. Why repeat others' errors? And fact-checking is so easy these days, right?

It's also important for a local guide to keep current, especially a city guide in a metropolis that reinvents itself at a bewildering pace. Los Angeles is a great example. The changes that have occurred in just a few years are enough to make your head spin. Here are just a handful:

- Remember The Source, the restaurant used as a location in the Woody Allen movie *Annie Hall*, where Woody's character, Alvy, orders alfalfa sprouts and a plate of mashed yeast? Its name was changed to the

Cajun Bistro and then to Cabo Cantina. Or at least it was called that the last time I looked. Next time I do an L.A. city tour, I will certainly run down there and check.

- The legendary Ambassador Hotel, home of the Cocoanut Grove nightclub, host to six Academy Award ceremonies and the site of Robert Kennedy's assassination in 1968, was torn down in 2005 despite strenuous preservation efforts. A school complex has been built on the site.

- Frank Gehry's Walt Disney Concert Hall, just a parking garage and a stalled construction site when I began guiding in Los Angeles, is now one of the world's most famous and most frequently photographed buildings.

- In addition to buildings that have been built, rebuilt, renamed, or torn down, there are places that never were, like the opening location for *77 Sunset Strip*. It was really 8524 Sunset, Dino's Lodge, which no longer exists. But there's a plaque on the sidewalk commemorating the old TV series, which ran from 1958 to 1964. If you're guiding folks of a certain age, just start singing the theme and snapping your fingers as you drive along the Strip west of La Cienega. They'll soon be singing and snapping right along with you! (You're too young to remember the tune? No problem. It's on YouTube, of course.)

- And don't forget, celebrities are always adding their handprints and footprints to the Forecourt at the Chinese Theatre, and new stars keep popping up on the Walk of Fame!

I could go on, but you get the idea. A great guide needs A Keen Desire to Keep On Learning Forever!

Like Leopards and Salesmen, You Need to Know Your Territory

Knowledge of the territory comes in two flavors: The Fun Stuff and the Practical Stuff. The Fun Stuff is your commentary, such as stories, jokes, and information about the wonderful sights you point out to people who have come to see and experience them. It's probably why you became a tour guide in the first place.

The Practical Stuff is important for your guests' comfort and safety. You probably have some valuable information your tour director would be grateful to hear, too, especially if he's a foreigner. I will discuss the tour director/tour guide relationship at length in the next section.

If you live in the city where you guide, you probably knew plenty of Fun Stuff before you began giving tours. Many a guide has entered the profession because friends and family kept saying, "It's such fun to visit you! You always show us such a great time and take us to all the best places. You should be a tour guide!"

If you're a tour director who also gives local city tours in the various countries where you travel or in other cities in your own country, you need to become an "honorary local" by learning as much about your temporary city as you can.

Here is a basic checklist of Things to Know for a standard city tour in a van or motor coach. The possibilities are endless, but this should get you started.

City Tour Fun Stuff

- Nicknames or alternate names for the city
- Information about the landmarks you will see and visit
- Size of the city, in area and in population
- Ethnic makeup of the city
- Lifestyles, languages, and customs of various groups who live there
- Cost of renting or buying a typical dwelling. What percentage of residents own their own homes?
- How much does gas (petrol) cost? Americans always want to know this, wherever they are in the world. I have no idea why, but they do.
- Famous people who were born there or live there
- History of the city. Who settled there and why? How did the location and its geographical features affect its settlement and development? For example, Manhattan is a tiny island. The only way to grow was up, enabled by solid bedrock and, eventually, skyscraper

technology. Boston, in contrast, spread out through land reclamation, doubling its size in the 19th century by filling in the Back Bay and other areas. Geography was destiny for New York and Boston, and dictated the shape of the cityscapes we see today. Many great cities have grown up on a river or upon a natural harbor.

- What is the city known for? Architectural treasures, historical events, a spectacular natural site, local industry, recreation, politics, institutes of higher education?

Sometimes I like to pick a theme for my city tour, especially if I have an audience with a specialized interest. The movie industry is an obvious theme for a Los Angeles tour and I often use it. I don't announce the theme to the group; it's just in the back of my mind for my own amusement and organizational purposes.

Once I was assigned a group of mayors from other cities. For them, I chose water as my theme. Why? Because I don't know much about politics, but I do know that there is no subject more political in Southern California than water rights!

Without imported water, there would be no Los Angeles. From the city's founding upon *El Rio de Porciúncula* to the move from the river's flooded banks; from the era of the *zanjero* (water-ditch tender, who was so important he was paid more than the mayor) to L.A.'s first water war (in 1810, the city successfully sued the padres of the San Fernando

Mission for damming the river); from William Mulholland's notorious diversion of water from the Owens Valley so he could build the Los Angeles Aqueduct to today's environmental efforts to restore natural vegetation along the river's concrete channel and other ongoing political maneuvering – any civic leader can relate to the bitter power struggle over water in Los Angeles.

It also makes a great tour theme, because the idea of water is everywhere in the city, even in the names of streets. Rodeo Drive comes from the original name of the rancho that became Beverly Hills, *El Rodeo de las Aguas* (the gathering of the waters). These waters flowed down from Coldwater Canyon and other streams and created *La Cienega* (the swamp). You can still see one of the old *zanjas* (water ditches) at Olvera Street. Downtown, you can't miss the landmark Department of Water and Power Building, encircled by a pool that is part of the air-conditioning and heating system. Fountains are everywhere in Los Angeles, many of them alluding to the arid city's thirst. Robert Graham's Source Figure, a serene nude African-American in bronze, seems to be offering water from her cupped hands to all who mount Downtown's Bunker Hill Steps. Atop the Electric Fountain in Beverly Hills is a kneeling Native American, perhaps praying for rain or thanking the gods for the water splashing around him and into his outstretched hands.

The theme concept has helped me organize commentary for city tours in cities I've never lived in and have to discover primarily through research rather than experience.

The history of Helsinki, for instance, works well for me as the tour theme for that little gem of a city. I begin by telling my group that the history of Finland and its capital is very simple: first it was Swedish, then it was Russian, and now it is Finnish. The motto for the early Finnish nationalists was *Swedes we are not, Russians we will never be, so let us therefore be Finns.* In the next few hours, I flesh out that concept as we drive through Helsinki, observing that practically everything around us relates to its fascinating history, which turns out not to be so simple after all.

The modern Finnish city is full of historic reminders. The street signs are bilingual – Finnish and Swedish. You can attend plays in Swedish at the Swedish National Theatre and in Finnish at the Finnish National Theatre. There's a statue commemorating Johan Ludvig Runeberg, Finland's national poet. Below him is the Muse of Poetry, holding a scroll with the words to the Finnish National Anthem, which Runeberg wrote – in Swedish! (Do you know of any other national anthem that's written in a foreign language?)

Parts of Helsinki look very Russian. During the early 19th century, the architect Carl Ludvig Engel designed many buildings in both St. Petersburg and Helsinki. The enormous Russian-Byzantine Uspenski Cathedral would look right at home in Moscow. Hollywood has often taken advantage of these Russian aspects of the cityscape. Helsinki's lovely Senate Square, as a stand-in for St. Petersburg, co-starred with Warren Beatty in *Reds*. Part of the classic film *Dr. Zhivago* was shot in the city and elsewhere in Finland. The movie *Gorky Park* was filmed not in Moscow, where the actual Gorky Park is, but in Helsinki.

I have found that a broad theme like this can help with the pacing of a tour, giving it a nice flow and a solid foundation for all the rest of your Fun Stuff.

City Tour Practical Stuff

Now we come to the nuts and bolts of a city tour: the Practical Stuff. Some of the following information you will receive from whoever has hired you, some from the tour director, if there is one, and some from your own research.

Schedule: How long is the tour? Three to four hours is typical for a half-day city tour, but it could be ninety minutes or less, or a full day.

Routing: Where do you start and where do you end? A city tour can begin anywhere – from the airport, a cruise ship terminal, or whatever hotel your clients are staying in. Be prepared with your commentary accordingly. For example, when my L.A. city tour begins at the Roosevelt Hotel, in the heart of Hollywood and legendary site of the first Academy Awards ceremony, I start talking movies and pointing out Tinseltown landmarks immediately. When the group is staying in Pasadena for the Rose Bowl, it's about twenty-five minutes on the freeway from the hotel to Hollywood, so I'm free to begin the tour in a more general way.

A tour often ends back at its starting point, but sometimes it doesn't. If you've left your car there and need to get back to it, the company should reimburse expenses for your cab fare or whatever arrangements you need to make to be reunited with your vehicle. Sometimes the coach driver can take you back.

Is anything happening that might affect your planned route, such as road closures, construction, a parade, a demonstration, a holiday, a festival, a film shoot? Be sure your routing is legal and safe as well as interesting, and adjust your timing if you expect delays due to any of these factors. Avoid backtracking whenever possible.

Itinerary: What's included? If the tour brochure has promised the clients that they will "see" something, you must at least drive by it. If they have been told they will "visit," then you will get off the coach and go into the place.

On my first trip to Riga, Latvia, I took a Jewish Heritage tour that the American travel company I worked for was interested in offering the following year. In town, the group visited the active synagogue, the ruins of a Great Choral Synagogue, and a small museum. Then we drove for about half an hour to Rumbala Forest, where we were supposed to visit a Holocaust memorial dedicated to the 25,000 Latvian Jews who were massacred there. Imagine my astonishment when, upon reaching a large sculpture that marks the entrance to the forest, I heard the guide tell the driver, "All right, they've seen it, now turn around and go back to the city. I've got another group at 5:00 o'clock."

Needless to say, I didn't recommend him to my company. The group *saw* Rumbala Forest and the entrance to it, yes, but we were supposed to *visit* the entire site.

The following year we used our own handpicked guide, and you can be sure that all my groups walked into the memorial. Rumbala Forest is one of the most powerful and moving Holocaust remembrance sites I have ever experienced. Every time we visited, I felt sorry for the people short-changed by the guide who did not allow them to bear witness.

Stops: Check beforehand to be sure each attraction you plan to visit is open or if there are any restrictions you should know about, such as timed entry and/or exit, metal detectors, prohibitions on large bags or backpacks, rules for photography (fee required, flash not allowed, or no cameras at all), partial closure of the site, any hazards due to construction, etc.

Is there any special insider information to share with the tour director? I have always been most grateful to the Moscow guide who taught me which guards to bribe, and the going rate, to get my group into Lenin's Tomb without having to stand in line for an hour and a half. (It was worth every ruble.)

Know when opening time is. In Washington, D.C., the company's memo told me to have my group lined up and ready to enter the National Cathedral at 9:30. My local guide, a sweet old gentleman whose commentary and delivery were spectacularly boring, completely redeemed himself in my eyes when he warned me that the Cathedral opened at 10:00 and not a minute sooner. He also knew that if we left as instructed at 4:15 for our 4:30 tour of the Capitol, we'd be late and our appointment would be cancelled. So we departed at 4:00 and made it on time. I was told in no uncertain terms by the Capitol authorities that we would indeed have been cancelled if we'd arrived any later.

Some places change their opening hours by the season, so check for periodic updates. Attractions such as fountains are often seasonal, too. My group at Longwood Gardens missed the fountain show by one day, but they didn't care because the gardens and Conservatory alone are worth the price of admission. Mainly they didn't care, though, because our gardener/guide didn't say, "What a pity you couldn't have come next week!" Remember Rule #1: *This Is the Best of All Possible Tours?* Of course you do.

Know if there is an admission fee and be prepared to pay it and pick up tickets if required. Know if there are any fees for parking at the attraction, or any restrictions on parking or drop-off in the area. The driver should know this, but it never hurts if the guide does, too.

Comfort stops: Most importantly, *always know where the toilets are!* One of my favorite guides in South Africa refers to rest stops as "Splash 'n' Dash."

Restaurants: If lunch is included, either you or the tour director will make the appropriate arrangements. In either case, find out what's included on the menu. Be sure not to tell the guests about any delicious local or seasonal specialties if they aren't going to be able to order them! However, if you're stopping in a likely place long enough for a snack and your city is known for its street food (churros at L.A.'s Olvera Street, anyone?), by all means mention it.

Emergencies: Know where the urgent care clinics and hospitals and 24-hour pharmacies are, just in case. If your group is from out of the country, have the contact information for their local embassy or consulate on hand. If *you* are from out of the country, a tour director, say, who is giving tours as an "honorary local" in a city and country you don't live in, be sure you know the local number for emergencies. In the U.S. and Canada, for example, it's 911; in most of Europe it's 112. It takes only a few moments to look up emergency numbers and put them into your phone. You'll be glad you did.

I'm forever grateful to two heroic guides I worked with many times in Vilnius, Lithuania. One day, after Dalija and Egli had finished giving their usual walking tours and we were about to depart Vilnius for lunch, touring with Dalija in another town and then on to the airport, one of my guests fell and cut her forehead badly. While I grabbed two doctors and a nurse who happened to be in the group to help me stop the bleeding, Dalija called an ambulance, which took Sue to the emergency hospital. Dalija also called Egli, who was on her way home, finished for the day, or so she thought. Dalija and I continued with the tour, while Egli drove to the hospital to assist Sue, who received fourteen stitches but nevertheless was determined to fly on to Moscow with us. So Egli took her to a late lunch and then brought her to meet us at the airport for our evening flight.

It's especially great that Egli was able to go to the hospital and translate for my guest, because the only Lithuanian I can ever remember is *ačiū,* which is pronounced *achoo,* just like a sneeze. It means *thank you.* The help I got from my guides that day was nothing to sneeze at, but you can believe I said a heartfelt *ačiū!* to them both.

Weather: Is your city known for sudden downpours when you least expect it, right out of a clear blue sky? (Innsbruck, I'm looking at *you.*) Warn the nice folks. Better yet, tell the tour director in advance, if he's new to your fair city, so he can warn his passengers in time to bring along their little travel umbrellas.

Best Friends Forever, at Least for a Few Hours

This leads us to an important source of knowledge and a critical part of giving a city tour: communicating with the tour director about how the day will go. If she's someone you work with regularly, a brief text, call, or email a night or two before the tour to touch base and get any special requests should suffice. (She should have reconfirmed with you, but if she didn't, you do it.)

One year I gave a series of L.A. city tours for several British groups who were on a round-the-world journey. When I asked their tour director if there was anything special I should know about the group, she reported, "Coming in from Fiji at 2:30, cranky, hungry, and exhausted!" So the first thing I always said to them was, "Wow! You just flew in all the way from Fiji? How do you manage to look so good?"

If it's your first time with this tour director or this company, here are some issues to clarify:

If there are any paid attractions on the tour, who pays, you or the tour director? Are you supposed to get tickets in advance?

Is there a meal included in the tour? What is the menu? Which of you will reconfirm with the restaurant?

How long will the group be in the city? Do they have free time? How much? Are any meals not included while the group is in town? Find out if it's all right to mention any of the following in your commentary:

- Attractions and activities not on the tour. Before my San Diego assignments, I was specifically instructed to tell the passengers that they could return to Coronado via ferry or taxi to visit the Hotel del Coronado during their free time. Many were disappointed that buses were no longer allowed to stop at the hotel, so they were happy to learn that they could visit this landmark Victorian resort on their own.

- Where and how to shop and what local specialties to look for. Does one bargain, or are prices fixed? By the way, I've often heard guides and travelers alike confuse *bargaining* with *bartering. Bargaining* means trying to get something for a lower price. *Bartering* is the exchange of goods for other goods rather than for money. *Hello, Madam! I like your shoes, Madam! I'll trade you this handmade bowl for those shoes, Madam!*

- Restaurant recommendations; any special local or seasonal foods to try

- How to get around the city: how much taxis cost, how local transportation works and how to buy bus, trolley, subway, or ferry tickets. Do you get them in advance or on board?
- Any special sports events, performances, or holiday events and how to procure tickets

If your job includes recommending and selling optional excursions, by all means go ahead and sell. Just be sure to find out first if the group has time to take advantage of your offerings.

If all their time in your city is fully booked, or if they are on their way out of town right after you leave them, stick to what they are seeing and experiencing with you. Avoid allowing them that awful feeling that they're going to miss something wonderful. Remember Rule #1: *This Is the Best of All Possible Tours!*

Usually it's the tour director's responsibility to brief his passengers on practical survival information, but if the group has just arrived in your country, you might ask if he'd like you to tell them where to change money, if tap water is safe to drink, or anything else they may need to know.

And We're Off!

Spot time is when you are supposed to report for duty. You show up a little *before* your official spot time, which is usually about thirty minutes before the tour begins. You are dressed appropriately in a sharp blazer and crisp pants or equally suitable attire, looking like a million bucks waiting for change. You are also wearing your best asset, a big confident smile.

You are squeaky clean and smell lovely, but without the aid of cologne, perfume, or scented aftershave, of course. So many people have allergies these days.

Your deodorant is also of the scentless variety. When I was a teenager, back when dinosaurs roamed the earth, I read all the teen beauty magazines avidly and have never forgotten one column, under the heading of Deodorant, which said, simply, "You are not the one girl in a thousand who doesn't need one. Use it." Sage advice for all tour guides, too. That goes double for breath freshener.

You find the coach and reserve your seat behind the driver or across from him, depending on where the mike is, with your nice professional-looking "Reserved for Tour Guide" sign. Or you can always just throw your bag on the seat, if it's a nice big bag with nothing terribly valuable in it. Introduce yourself to the driver, if you haven't worked with him before, and exchange cell numbers before you do anything else.

You check the microphone, or perhaps you've brought your own. If you've never worked with this tour director before, or if you have and you know she tends to forget this little detail, sneak a quick peek into the on-board toilet for cleanliness and plenty of toilet paper. And be sure it's open, or that you know where the key is. It's not really your job, and most city tours make sufficient toilet stops, but you never know. One time in Moscow, I had a passenger who was suffering from a common tourist complaint and needed constant access to a toilet throughout the city tour. Of course he should have stayed at the hotel, but he wasn't about to miss Moscow, despite feeling rotten. The WC was locked and we couldn't find the key anywhere, but the driver was resourceful. He whipped out a knife with a six-inch blade and forced the lock with it. (Naturally, this particular driver's name was Vladimir. For the rest of the day I couldn't stop thinking about Vlad the Impaler.)

You have a chat with the driver and the tour director, making sure you're all on the same page concerning the itinerary, length of the tour, and the number and timing of stops. If it's been your job to prepare the routing, which is usually the case, sometimes with input from the tour director or the company, give it to the driver with a map. Be sure he understands it and has no objections to anything. If he tells you his bus is too tall to get under a bridge or too heavy to go over one that's on your route, he has the final say. Safety first!

If the driver tells you he's also a driver/guide and does this route all the time and doesn't need to discuss anything, you can tactfully say something like, "I'm sure you know this city like the back of your hand, but let's just check this routing together. This tour director might want us to do it a little differently." If you get the feeling you might have an egotist on your hands, you might add, "Listen, I know you could give all the commentary and I'm sure your tour is great. You probably know a lot more than I do. If I say anything you think is wrong, please let me know, but not in front of the passengers. OK?"

My own experience with problem drivers? Really rare. On the other hand, I can't begin to count the number of times a driver has gotten me out of some trouble or other. Georg and Ivan, a couple of drivers you will meet in the next section, are just two of the great colleagues out of dozens that I could mention.

The driver may be a native, or he may never have seen the city in his life. If the latter is the case, you will need to direct him.

There are two basic ways to direct a driver, and it's a good idea to ask which one he prefers. You can lean over and quietly say, "Take the next right," or "Go up the hill and then turn left at the light." Or you can say, on the mike, "Now, ladies and gentlemen, as Bob makes this right turn, on your left you will see our magnificent new cathedral," or "and as Bob goes up this hill and turns left, be sure to be looking to your right for your first view of the spectacular Walt Disney Concert Hall!"

The only difficulty with this second method is that you have to be darn sure that Bob is willing to hang on your every word of commentary.

I like to mix the two techniques, if the driver is amenable. When the turns and landmarks are coming thick and fast, it's easier to just hiss, "Next left!" "Right at the light!" but it's also nice to involve the driver in your commentary when you can. Always call him by name; never refer to him in front of your passengers just as "the driver." Some guides call the driver "our Coach Captain," or similar nickname, which is fun, and is also a respectful way to acknowledge the person who, after all, is doing an essential job. The tour couldn't go on without him!

Clarify roles: It's a good idea to discuss who does what with the tour director, if you think there might be any doubt.

Who does the overview of the day? Either or both of you could do this. Sometimes tour directors like to share a few highlights of the tour with their group before turning over the mike. If so, you can certainly say, "As Leslie mentioned, first we're going to see...." Then continue with your commentary.

Who counts the passengers after each stop? I was trained that the tour director does, and I would feel very uncomfortable if I didn't, but I've worked with guides in several countries who have obviously been told that it was *their* job and who absolutely insist on doing the counting. In that case, I go ahead and count and let the guide do it, too. An extra count never hurts, and the last thing you want in front of a group is a battle of wills. If you both count, take a moment to plan your choreography so you don't bump into each other walking down the aisle.

Who announces the stops? Usually that's the guide's job, after finding out how the tour director wants the tour to run. Once he makes his wishes known, you are in charge. Before making a stop, tell the group what time to be back, not just how long they have. At the first stop, synchronize watches. "We'll have half an hour here. My watch says 11:15. Please be back at 11:45."

Yes, I know, hardly anybody wears watches any more. If *you* do, make sure your watch is correct, because most of your passengers will be checking their phones for the time, and they will be right!

When announcing a photo stop, you probably won't want to say how long the stop will be; usually it's better just to play it by ear. However, it's important to avoid calling it a "quick stop," even if that's exactly how you're thinking of it. If the passengers hear "OK, we're going to make a quick photo stop" several times in a day, they might feel rushed, whether you are actually rushing them or not!

So how do you get them back if you haven't announced a definite time? The best technique I know is to ask the driver to turn off the engine when you arrive at the stop. When you want to depart, ask her to turn the engine on again. Most of your passengers will get the hint and hop back on board right away. You can round up any others by walking up to them and offering them a polite invitation to re-board the coach.

A tour director will often need to take the mike for a few minutes at the end of a city tour or the conclusion of a day's travel, so he can give logistical information to the group. Generally the tour director will let you know if he'd like to do this and how much time he needs, but if he doesn't mention it, ask him. It's a nice thing to do and will endear you to your colleague, who may be new at this, or may simply have forgotten that this is his last chance to remind the group that they need to have bags ready at 7:00 am.

Sometimes there is no tour director; you and the driver are in charge of the excursion alone. The tour director may be back at the hotel, dutifully marking luggage to be placed on the ship for the cruise portion of the tour or catching up on a mountain of paperwork. Or she may have decided to spend the afternoon by the pool, having a mai tai and a manicure. At any rate, you and the driver are on your own.

If that's the case, then you get to do both your job and the tour director's. You introduce yourself and the driver to the group. Perhaps you assist the driver by standing next to the back door of the coach, if there is one, to be sure the passengers get off and on safely. You announce the stops and the time to be back. You count, for sure. Twice.

At the end of the tour, give the passengers any logistical information that you may have been asked to give them, thank the driver, and remind your guests to check all around them and in the overhead for any belongings. (Cell phones in particular have a sneaky way of disappearing between the seats, and I'm always amazed at the number of people who forget to retrieve that little bag of T-shirts they bought for the grandkids.) Say goodbye to them as they get off, thank them for anything that they may press into your hand as they shake it, check the coach immediately after everyone has disembarked to be certain that nothing was left behind, and you're done.

Speaking of counting, you need to make sure you not only have the right *number* of people, but the right *people*. In a city like Los Angeles, for example, where there may be a dozen coaches lined up at Grauman's Chinese Theatre or Olvera Street, it's not uncommon for a dazed tourist to climb onto the wrong bus. (Of course *you* gave your people the bus number, but perhaps some other guide forgot.) You can't expect yourself to remember forty new faces that you've barely had a chance to glance at, but they should all recognize *you*. So when everyone is back on the coach, be sure to ask them if they do! You'd be amazed how many times one or two will scamper off the bus, embarrassed – but not nearly as embarrassed as you would be if you left one or two of your own passengers behind, helplessly wandering the streets like Neil Simon's *Out-of-Towners*. Or worse, confidently hopping into a taxi, doing the rest of the itinerary on their own, and meeting you back at the hotel, expecting you to reimburse them for the $60 cab fare.

The Tour Director as Honorary Local Guide, Unscheduled

Just as a guide sometimes works without a tour director, often a tour director works without a guide. If you're a tour director, you might even occasionally find yourself giving a city tour you had no idea you were going to give. I do, anyway. I'm always getting myself into some sort of trouble.

During the Passion Play year of 2010, I led a number of tours in Bavaria. We started in Munich and then drove a couple of hours to Oberammergau, where the play is held every ten years, and drove back to Munich the next day. On the way out, the group didn't get to see much of the city. My driver, Georg, a proud native of Munich, asked me if I wanted to take a different route on the return. He suggested that we swing around and come in from the north so that we could show them some of Munich's highlights: the Olympiapark, where the 1972 Summer Games were held; the futuristic BMW Museum and headquarters; the lively bohemian district of Schwabing; the historic buildings along Ludwigstrasse, one of Europe's most impressive thoroughfares; and more. I immediately said yes, which was rather daring as I'd never been to Munich before. But I couldn't resist. Exploring new places is such fun!

Georg whispered a cue to me as we approached each landmark. Then I surreptitiously glanced at my Munich guidebook for a few pertinent facts and threw in a comment or two from my own stock of Fun Stuff about the Olympics, Beemers, or Mad King Ludwig. I almost gave myself away when Georg identified the birthplace of the Empress Elizabeth of Austria and I squealed, "Sisi was born right *there? Really?*" I adore beautiful, tragic Sisi, the Princess Diana of the late nineteenth century. I could talk about Sisi for hours.

Despite that little slip, I think we fooled the passengers into thinking they'd gotten a proper city tour from two people who knew what they were doing, even though only one of us did. *Danke schön, Georg!*

Another helpful driver's knowledge rescued me one night in Moscow, when I ended up finishing a transfer from the airport for a local guide who had to hop off the bus early.

Between Sheremetyevo Airport and our downtown hotel are some of Moscow's most iconic landmarks. The 18-mile ride is a thrill for anyone seeing the city for the first time, especially at night, all lit up with neon, the spires of the Kremlin piercing the dark sky. On my fourth or fifth go-round of the season, the guide asked if I could let her off at a metro stop just outside the city. Our flight had arrived late, and if she were to take us all the way into town, she would miss the last train home, over an hour's ride out to the suburbs. What could I say? Yes, of course. She hopped off, and I took over the mike.

We turned into the Inner Ring, and I pointed out the State Duma, the Bolshoi, and the lovely Art Nouveau Hotel Metropole. When we passed a monumental auto showroom full of luxury cars for Moscow's billionaires, I borrowed some Fun Stuff from Gennady, one of the other guides who sometimes picked us up at the airport. "OK, let's read some Russian signs together. *Ma-se-ra-ti, Lam-bour-ghi-ni, Fer-ra-ri!*"

Gennady usually joked about the statue of Karl Marx in front of the showroom, too. "He destroyed our country, and what do we do? We build a monument to him." As an honorary local, I didn't think it would be very polite to say such a thing, so I came up with a joke of my own.

"On your right, Karl Marx." Pause. "Gee, you'd think he'd be on the left, wouldn't you?"

Believe it or not, this actually got a laugh. Encouraged, I dramatically pointed out the old KGB headquarters and again received a satisfying reaction from the group. Then

I got cocky. I started to describe a small monument that most of the guides who transferred us from the airport didn't even bother to mention, although Gennady had, once or twice.

"There on your left is a memorial in honor of the brave Russian soldiers who liberated the Bulgarians from…"

Uh-oh. Brain freeze. I couldn't remember. Not a clue. Then the driver, in a basso profundo that would have done credit to Boris Godunov, leaned over and intoned deeply to me from across the aisle,

"Tuuurks."

"…the brave Russian soldiers who liberated the Bulgarians from the Turks!" I said, triumphantly. *Spasibo bolshoe, Ivan!*

Now that we've got all this Knowledge, let's find out how to use it. On to *Technique!*

6

TECHNIQUE

———

Have you been wondering when we were going to get to Rule #3? Here it is:

> **RULE #3:**
> **POINT OUT WHAT'S OUT THE WINDOW**

At ITMI, tour guides are given a powerful image to remember: whenever you are with passengers in a van or motor coach, *you are the eyes for the people.* After all, you are sitting up front, next to the driver or just behind her, and you have the best view in the house. This is true whether driving across town or across country, but it's especially important to be hyper-alert during a city tour, where there are so many features of interest to point out and to talk about. In a sense, you are creating the cityscape before the eyes of your passengers as you explore it together, spinning your wonderful stories about public spaces and private buildings and the people who inhabit them.

It's a simple idea that is sometimes very difficult to put into practice. As a rookie, I kept looking to the right most of the time, because that's where I was sitting. I knew I had to cure myself of this bad habit after an incident one day in Hollywood during one of my first tours. We were approaching the Egyptian Theatre, which had just reopened after a major renovation. Originally built in 1922 by Sid Grauman for movie premieres, it was now the permanent home of American Cinematheque, a nonprofit organization dedicated to film and video.

"Coming up on your right," I announced enthusiastically, "is the Egyptian Theatre, a great example of historic preservation, part of our current efforts to revitalize Hollywood Boulevard and bring back the glamour of Hollywood's Golden Age. It was just restored to the tune of fourteen million dollars, but it was well worth it! Look at the pharaoh's head and the Egyptian paintings, and the walls that look like they're made of ancient stones from the pyramids. Notice how that line of palm trees leads you right into the forecourt...."

There was a collective gasp from everyone on the bus. My first thought was, *Wow, fantastic! These people are really into historic preservation!* Then I turned around and saw they were all looking to the left, where there was a big car accident.

Shortly after that embarrassing day, I saw a movie that had a lighthouse in it. *That's what I need to be like,* I thought, *a lighthouse beacon, searching to the left, searching to the right.* This image of constantly scanning the horizon helped me break the habit of looking just one way.

There are different techniques for pointing things out; whichever one works best for you is fine. You can say something is on the left or right, on the door side or the driver's side of the coach, or you can use the face of a clock. *One o'clock* or *two o'clock* would mean *coming up on your right* and *eleven o'clock* or *ten o'clock* means *coming up on your left*. *Three o'clock* and *nine o'clock* would indicate directly to the right or left, respectively. Naturally, those are the only positions you need because *twelve* is too soon and anything else is too late, as per Rule #3. If you've passed it, it's no longer out the window, right?

The *door side/driver side* technique is a boon to those who have trouble with right and left without staring at their hands for a couple of minutes. I have no sense of direction but I do know my right from my left, so I generally use that method, along with the clock on occasion. For example, I typically say something like, "Coming up on your left, at about eleven o'clock now...."

I once used the *door side/driver side* technique, but after a season in continental Europe, where one drives on the right, followed by several weeks in South Africa, where one drives on the left, and then back to Europe again, I discovered I was much more likely to mess up using *door side/driver side*. I gave up that method for good after leading my first cruise tour of Japan, which also visited one South Korean port. In Japan, traffic moves on the left; in South Korea, on the right. When the door side and driver side of the buses for our shore excursions changed places three times in as many days, I took a couple of aspirin, went back to *left/right*, and stayed there for the remainder of my guiding career.

Timing Is Everything: In Life, Comedy, and Tour Guiding

Timing is just as important to a tour guide as it is to a comedian, an essential part of your technique. You need to anticipate what's coming up before you actually see it. Whenever possible, start talking about a major landmark about half a block before you get to it, in order to have time to talk about it. Once it's behind you, let it go. Go on to the next one. If you miss anything you intended to mention, forgive yourself immediately, keep going, and above all don't apologize!

When landmarks come thick and fast, timing is tricky and takes a lot of practice. It's one of the two most challenging aspects of city guiding. The other major challenge, of course, is when you're stuck in traffic or in a relatively boring stretch and there's nothing to point out at the moment. Then you need to rely on a nice supply of filler: Fun Facts, a joke, a good story.

One technique that works well in some situations is to announce two, three, or even four upcoming landmarks, and talk a little about them just before you get there, preferably during one of those boring stretches. Then simply point them out as they whizz by.

Here's an example. Many times I've taken groups from Moscow to St. Petersburg by train, arriving around midnight at St. Petersburg's Moscow Railway Station. Our local guide for the next few days meets us on the platform, leads us to the coach, and guides us down St. Petersburg's main thoroughfare, Nevsky Prospekt, which is full of magnificent buildings, magically lit. It's technically just a simple, quick transfer to the hotel at a very late hour, not a real "tour," but it's also the first time my passengers are seeing one of the great cities of the world, and I want them to wake up and be thrilled. As we approach the Griboedov Canal, I know we've lucked into a guide who really cares about her job if I hear something like this:

"Soon we will cross a little bridge, and I want you to look very quickly to your right, down the canal. You will get a glimpse of the famous Church on Spilled Blood. We will visit it tomorrow, but tonight you can see it all lit up. Just after we cross the canal, keep looking to your right for the Art Nouveau House of Books, the old Singer Sewing Machine Company building, and then look immediately to your left for the Cathedral of Our Lady of Kazan. It has a curved colonnade and a great dome. Ready? Now! Look right, quick!"

Another, simpler way of dealing with an abundance of riches is to ask the driver to slow down. A cooperative driver will do the best she can without antagonizing all the drivers behind her. Or you might be able to pull over for a couple of minutes next to an especially interesting landmark that you have a lot to say about but are not visiting on the tour. Boston's Massachusetts State House; several homes in Newport, Rhode Island; and the Castle of Good Hope and the Company's Garden in Cape Town come to mind. Or you can always go around twice, as I do at the Boston Common and Public Garden. There's just too darn much to see and talk about on only one pass, unless the traffic is slow.

Incidentally, while we're on the subjects of Cape Town and Boston: in Cape Town, it's *Company's Garden*, not Company Gardens. And in Boston it's *Boston Common*, not Commons; and *Public Garden*, not Public Gardens or Boston Garden or Boston Gardens. Got it? Good. If you ever guide in either of those magnificent cities you will neatly avoid a really *common* mistake. (Sorry about the pun – it's a professional hazard.) I'm sure you can think of similar, frequently misnamed places to watch out for where you guide.

Suppose you have a juicy story about a landmark but no time to tell it while passing and no place to stop? Point it out and say, "See that building? I've got a special story about it to tell you, later on." Then, during one of those boring stretches, tell it.

Let's go back to Cape Town to illustrate this technique. Say you're leading a quick city tour on the way to the Cape Peninsula or the Winelands. You pick up your group at one of the posh hotels at the V&A Waterfront and almost immediately pass the Somerset Hospital, where a distinguished British Army physician named James Barry was posted for several years in the early 19th century. Barry was a brilliant surgeon, one of the first ever to perform a successful Caesarian, saving both mother and baby. He was exacting and argumentative, insisting on standards of hygiene and sanitation far in advance of normal practice for the time. Dr. Barry made enemies among the quack doctors and unlicensed pharmacists in the Cape Colony and challenged many a colleague to a duel. He was a strange little fellow, only five feet tall, and he had an odd, high-pitched voice, but he strutted around like he owned the place and carried the longest sword in town. He was also…a woman!

Barry disguised herself as a man when she entered medical school in Edinburgh at age 14 and managed to keep her secret until her death. The ruse enabled her to become the first woman in British history to study and practice medicine officially.

Great story, isn't it? Except there's no time to tell it while driving by Somerset Hospital, and you certainly don't want to pull over and stop in front of it for five minutes when you've just started the tour. And if you continue the story after you've passed the hospital and need to be talking about other landmarks coming up, you're breaking Rule #3: *Point Out What's Out the Window*. So what to do? Something like this:

"The building that looks like a castle is Somerset Hospital, named after Lord Charles Somerset, a governor of the Cape Colony in the early 19th century. It's been declared a national monument. Later on, I'll tell you an amazing story about one of the doctors who practiced at the Somerset almost two hundred years ago."

Then you keep the story to yourself until you pass another hospital or other visual reminder out in the countryside, or whenever you feel the need for a good yarn. This does not break Rule #3, which comes into play simply to make sure your guests don't miss hearing about anything interesting. And here is why Rule #3 is important.

Shortly after passing the hospital, you will get a great panoramic view of one of the world's most striking cityscapes, a cluster of buildings nestled at the foot of Table Mountain. If you're still talking about a 19th-century doctor, nobody will be listening, because everyone will be staring at the skyline of the City Bowl against the mountain, knocked out by its beauty and wondering what all those buildings are. And one of them holds an even better story than the adventures of Dr. James Barry.

So take advantage of the best view they will have of the most prominent and most important building on the skyline. Point out the massive City Hall. Ask if anybody recognizes it. Did they see it on television in 1990, when Nelson Mandela addressed an ecstatic crowd of over 50,000 from its main balcony upon his release from prison after twenty-seven years?

Yes, in a few moments you will drive right by City Hall, and you will of course mention it then as well, but the passengers can't see the balcony while driving underneath it, or much of the building at all. From a distance, they can see it clearly, they can snap a photo out the bus window, and they can get chills as they imagine themselves among those 50,000 cheering people on that historic day. Your great sense of timing has just given them one of the most emotionally powerful moments of their trip to South Africa.

Cape Town's City Hall is just one example of many I could choose, from anywhere on the globe. I'm sure you can think of landmarks in the places where you guide that are best pointed out and spoken about at a distance, for two reasons: it's the best view of them, and you have time to talk about them.

Let's go back to Los Angeles for another example. I would first point out the city's tallest building from the Hollywood Freeway, where it towers over the rest of the skyline. On a stretch of highway with nothing in particular to the right or left, there is time to tell a lovely story about how it came to be built. The building is called the U.S. Bank Tower, formerly owned by a different bank and known as the First Interstate World Center. But its original name was the Library Tower.

In many large cities, the height of individual buildings is restricted, but a structure's "air rights," permission to use the vertical space above an existing low-rise building, can be bought and sold. After a terrible arson fire in 1986, the Los Angeles Central Library, a 1926 masterpiece designed by architect Bertram Goodhue, desperately needed money to restore the damaged structure and replace the lost books. A developer desperately wanted to build a massive skyscraper across the street. So the city allowed the library to sell its unused air rights to the tower's developer. The library used the money to restore the original building, construct a splendid eight-story annex, and buy a lot of books; the developer was legally enabled to erect the tallest building west of the Mississippi; and Los Angeles guides got a great story to tell.

So tell it on the freeway, when you have plenty of time. Later, when you pass between the skyscraper and the magnificently restored library right across from it, just remind your passengers how Los Angeles benefited from the clever deal that saved one historic landmark and created another. (We all still call it the Library Tower, by the way. But you also need to know its current official name, whether or not you care which bank owns it this week.)

I would also point out the Capitol Records building in Hollywood from the freeway, which again not only gives my guests the best view of the tower but gives me a chance to share with them the delightful tale of its creation.

Louis Naidorf was a 24-year-old architect working for Welton Becket Associates when he got an assignment to design a building for a top-secret client. All he was told was that they wanted lots of individual offices. Naidorf thought a cylindrical building would work nicely and give every office a view. When the client saw Naidorf's drawing, he was furious, thinking that Capitol's secret was out and the young architect was having a bit of a joke at their expense by designing a building that looked like a stack of records. Fortunately, higher-ups at Capitol decided it was a superb idea, and the iconic round tower still looks as fresh and playful today as it did when it was built in the 1950s.

Another critical aspect of technique is to pace your commentary to keep your audience interested and to avoid listener fatigue. On a half-hour transfer from the airport or a short city tour, you will be speaking most of the time. Be sure to pause for at least a few seconds every now and then! On a longer tour, give their ears (and your voice) an occasional rest. You can always ask if there are any questions. If there are, you've been given permission to continue talking.

In general, the longer the tour, the more pauses you need and the longer they can be. I once rode on a five-hour tour of the Big Island of Hawaii. The guide never once stopped speaking, but I stopped listening at about the three-hour mark. My brain shut down and I simply could not hear another word.

The opposite extreme is exemplified by a guide I sometimes worked with in Innsbruck, who clammed up every time the coach stopped at a light. He seemed to have no idea that his listeners might enjoy some interesting filler information rather than just sitting there waiting for the light to change. I used to pretend my guests had asked me questions about Austria and fed them to him. *Hans, someone just asked – please tell us about the school system here! Hey, Hans, how much snow do you get here in the winter?*

One of the best techniques for keeping people's ears attuned to you is to ask them questions from time to time. Sometimes I start off with one.

"What a beautiful day it is for our Los Angeles city tour today! Such a clear blue sky! Of course you know that L.A. used to be infamous for smog, but in recent years, we've done a marvelous job of cleaning up our air. By the way, does anybody know the date of the first smog report in Los Angeles?"

People guess all sorts of dates: when automobiles were invented, or when weather reports were first given on radio, or on television. Do you know? The answer might surprise you.

In 1542, Juan Rodriguez Cabrillo, a Portuguese explorer sailing for Spain, sighted what is now Santa Monica from near present-day Catalina Island. He noticed the smoke from the native inhabitants' campfires that hung in the air, trapped by the natural inversion layer created by the surrounding mountains, and he promptly named the place *La Bahía de los Fumos* – the Bay of Smokes. So the first smog report for Los Angeles was in 1542!

This technique works well because you're starting off with a Fun Fact and getting your group involved right away. You are also expressing enthusiasm and civic pride for your beloved city, illustrating how it is successfully dealing with a challenge that's been there forever.

What defines your city? What's a fun question you can start off with?

Now let's see how *Technique* leads to *Style* – to the development of your own unique voice.

7

A PERSONAL STYLE
ALL YOUR OWN

———

Whatever You Do, Kid, Always Serve It
with a Little Dressing
(George M. Cohan to Spencer Tracy)

Artistic style emerges from technique. Louis Naidorf's years of technical study and his sense of fun led him to a wonderfully creative place when he drew his round tower. Actors and musicians work for years to perfect their technique. They never stop practicing, so that they can continue to grow artistically.

Guides are performing artists, just as actors and musicians are. If you have solid guiding technique, you can relax and open yourself up to inspiration. You will be ready to be creative with your work, just like any other performer. Then your personal style and your own unique voice can emerge, and you'll always be able to "serve it with a little dressing," like Spencer Tracy or any other great actor. This may take time and plenty of trial and error. Have fun with the process, and don't be afraid to steal from others. Ironically, this tactic will help you develop your own style. Just be sure to steal from the best!

Originality Is the Art of Concealing Your Sources (Benjamin Franklin)

I think the good Dr. Franklin really meant that we all depend on others for our inspiration. I'm happy to give credit to one of my favorite sources to steal from, the best tour guide who doesn't actually give tours that I know: the legendary Hall of Fame broadcaster Vin Scully.

When Vin calls a Dodgers game, as he has done since 1950, millions of people hear him, but he sounds as if he's speaking to me alone. I'm sure all his other listeners feel the same way. He speaks casually, conversationally, confidingly. His love for the game shines through. When he says, "It's time for Dodger baseball!" or "Pull up a chair; we're just starting," you can tell he can't wait to see what's going to happen on the field this time and to share the magic of it all with his audience. He has been praised by countless critics for his eloquence, sense of humor, knowledge, enthusiasm, classiness, timing, and his uncanny ability to paint you a word picture of what's happening. In other words, the ideal tour guide!

One evening, while watching a game and basking in the warmth of Vin's voice, I decided to analyze his technique. Other sportscasters are capable, knowledgeable, and enthusiastic. Why has Vin Scully won all the awards? Why is he so beloved by millions? And how does he get me to imagine that I am the only person in the world listening to him at that moment?

I noticed that he often addresses the audience, saying things like, "Put him in the pitcher's spot, if you're scoring," or "You might be interested to know that his name means *owl* in Swedish," or "Text us your answer; we'd like to know your thinking on that." He might say, "With a runner on third, we always check – he does *not* have a wild pitch," or "Everyone in the ball park is looking bunt right now." He signs off with, "*Gooood* night, everybody!"

Vin draws us right into the press box with him by saying *you, we, everybody*. But I believe I discovered the secret of his special technique when I noticed what he *doesn't* say. Vin avoids phrases such as *any of you, some of you, many of you, all of you fans*.

When you send an email to more than one person, you are thinking about several people, but each person in that group reads your email as an individual. I hate getting messages that say, "Looking forward to seeing many of you there." *Many of me? How many of me are there?* "Maybe some of you haven't heard the news. I got married!" *Some of me? Which part of me?* It's much nicer to read "Hope to see you there" or "If you haven't heard the news, guess what? I got married!"

It's not hard to restructure a sentence to avoid *some of you* and its cousins while guiding:

> *Are any of you taking the optional tour?*
> *Is anyone taking the optional tour?*

Some of you have to leave tomorrow.
Some of us have to leave tomorrow.

Some of you may be wondering why the schedule was changed.
You may be wondering why the schedule was changed.

Many of you are going to the show. I have your tickets.
If you're going to the show, I have your ticket.

All of you guys are real troupers!
Everybody here is a real trouper!

The best tour companies urge their staff to treat everyone in the group as the individuals they are to the fullest extent possible. Doesn't the second example in each pair sound more personal than the first? When you're a member of an audience or a group, wouldn't you rather be addressed as an individual?

Whenever I'm with a tour group, I think of Vin Scully and try to be as warm, enthusiastic, and personal as he is. I will never be as knowledgeable about anything as Vin is about baseball. But I know where to steal great ideas!

Incidentally, I would advise against the use of "you guys," as in the last example above, not only because it's collective rather than personal, but because some adult women find it annoying to be addressed as "guys." If you and your group are very young, however, it's probably all right, especially if the group is all male. Just be sure it's not a habit you can't break if you work with older clients as well as student groups!

If you are guiding in a venue that dictates your style and even provides you with a script, such as a Living History park or program, you can still put your individual stamp on your character. On a trip to Australia many years ago, we visited Sovereign Hill in Ballarat, a re-creation of the gold-rush days of the 1850s. Our costumed guide carefully wrote out my certificate of participation with a feather quill pen and asked if I was *Miss* or *Mrs.* My stated preference for *Ms.* was met with a frown and a stern lecture informing me that there was no such title, and that I must truly be demented to think such a thing. She stayed in character throughout this scolding so perfectly that I got the giggles. She served up what was probably a canned script, but she served it with a nice little dollop of her own home-made dressing! Twenty years later, this delightful guide is my fondest memory of Ballarat.

The more you adopt a casual, conversational style when giving commentary on the motor coach rather than delivering a lecture on wheels, the longer you'll keep the interest and attention of your listeners. Have you noticed the relaxed, informal tone in my examples throughout this guide? Have you noticed the *Enthusiasm?*

8

PASSIONATE ENTHUSIASM

———

Nothing Great Was Ever Achieved Without Enthusiasm (Ralph Waldo Emerson)

If you love the places where you guide, your enthusiasm will show naturally. And of course you love your territory, right? Or do you? Do you find yourself sometimes feeling bored or angry? Do you have trouble not letting it show?

Enthusiasm is no problem for a beginner. You were probably so excited on that first tour that you had to make yourself breathe deeply so you didn't pop the buttons on your blazer. By the tenth time, you had it down like a real pro. But by the sixtieth time....

Perhaps you have been guiding in the same place for many years and it's become just another job. But retirement is not an option; you've got bills to pay! In that case, you have some work to do to rediscover what it was that inspired you when you began your career.

Was it the place itself? Then dig deeper and discover new and exciting things about it. Challenge yourself to add one new Fun Fact or anecdote to your commentary each time you guide. Was it the fun of being the storyteller, that smart, clever guy with the mike? Then resolve to tell a new joke to each new group. Was it your joy in sharing a place you love with others who are seeing it for the first time? Then your burnout cure is easy.

Remember what I consider the most important quality for a tour guide? It's at the top of my list at the beginning of this book. We've come full circle, right back to Empathy.

Just pick out one of your guests, someone whose face appeals to you. Like a parent with a young child just learning to walk, relive the joy of discovery through that special person. Think how happy she is, seeing all the wonderful things you are showing her! Then smile at the other people in the group, imagining their pleasure in what you are showing them. Everyone in the group will catch your enthusiasm and you will relive the travel experience through their eyes like a doting parent watching her toddler explore a fascinating new world. Your apathy will disappear like magic!

Now that we've gone through our list of the qualities that make a great tour guide with an emphasis on city tours, let's look at some other guiding scenarios. Of course, a guide in any situation needs the qualities we've discussed, but there are additional factors that may crop up when leading a walking tour or when traveling with a group for several days.

9

WALKING TOURS

I Can't Hear You; I'm Looking in the Wrong Direction

Unless you're required to wear a uniform, typically you can dress a bit less formally when giving a walking tour than on a city motor-coach tour. The most critical bits of apparel are good walking shoes and sun protection. You might wear a fun cap or hat with the name of your city or country on it. Guides in Salzburg or Munich delight their groups when they show up wearing traditional *Dirndln* or *Lederhosen*. The important thing is not to distract from what you are showing and telling the people.

I have worked many times with a lovely guide in Tallinn, Estonia, a tall, slender young woman who always dressed appropriately. Imagine my surprise one warm day when she met my group at the ferry terminal wearing a thin, low-cut blouse, and quite obviously braless! The driver and I had to take the luggage to the hotel while the group toured Tallinn with the guide on foot. When I met them afterwards, I asked how they had enjoyed it. One of the gentlemen spoke for all the men when he answered, "Honey, I sure *enjoyed* it, but I didn't hear a single *word* that girl said!" It's nice to be memorable, but you want to be remembered for the right reasons.

Good technique on a walking tour primarily requires that everyone can hear you. Audio listening devices are often used on walking tours and in museums these days, and they can certainly make your job easier. You can walk slowly and talk at the same time, turning around and checking periodically to give keen photographers and other stragglers a chance to catch up.

Be sure your mike is positioned so that if you turn your head, the mike comes with you. Elementary? I have worked with several guides who resist using listening devices and suffer from severe cases of mike drift. If you have been guiding for decades without these new-fangled gismos and find them challenging, practice with a mirror. Does your attitude toward them need adjusting? Remind yourself how much less wear and tear on your vocal cords there will be. Think how much money you will save on throat lozenges!

If you are guiding without amplification, you will need to walk to a spot and wait until everyone is there and in a position to hear you before you begin talking. Suppose one or two enthusiastic folks dog your every step and ask questions before the others are there? By all means, chat with them individually while walking or waiting for the rest of the group, but don't cut your commentary short. If you've already told these enthusiasts something you planned to tell everyone, tell it again to the entire group. The enthusiasts won't mind. They'll feel smart that they already knew what you were going to say!

When guiding outdoors, find shady spots whenever possible, and stand so that the group is not looking directly into the sun. This may sound basic, but many guides forget this courtesy. If you are forced to face the sun to spare your guests from the glare, I hereby give you permission to keep your sunglasses on. Whenever possible, it's a nice gesture to remove them for better eye contact with your group, but as one with sun-sensitive eyes and skin, I generally keep mine on and hope my enthusiastic smile and scintillating commentary will make up for it.

10

MULTI-DAY TOURS

———

If you are a national guide traveling with a group for several days, your relationship with the tour director is even more critical than it is on a city tour or a one-day excursion. The guests should see you as a team of two equals, with different responsibilities, who really enjoy each other's company. I'm sure one of the reasons that the Japanese students I guided for three days in Los Angeles had so much fun while being perfectly well behaved is that their teacher and I liked and respected each other so much. As a tour director, I've had the joy of working with wonderful national guides in many countries, from two days to more than two weeks. Good communication from the start is the key to a successful collegial relationship.

Here's an example of good communication. If the tour company or ground operator has given you copies of the schedule for all the passengers, resist the impulse to hand them out right away. Clear it with the tour director beforehand. He might think of it first and ask you to wait, especially if he sees you standing there holding a stack of paper. However, he may be too busy dealing with luggage or customs or an emergency, or perhaps he is too inexperienced to be aware that there might be a problem with dueling itineraries. So be sure to say, "This is the schedule that they've given me for the next couple of days. Shall I hand it out to your passengers or would you like to make changes?"

I learned the importance of this the hard way on my first arrival at Victoria Falls Airport in Zimbabwe, where I was unavoidably detained getting our bags through customs. It was a time of terrible shortages of staples, let alone luxuries, for the good people of Zim. I had brought bags full of candy to distribute, having been told by colleagues that it would be much appreciated by airport personnel and baggage handlers and could greatly expedite the process of getting my guests' bags through customs. In exchange for these rare treats, I would be given a group clearance and the guests could walk right through.

This proved to be true, but it wasn't necessarily any faster. Everyone working in the arrivals area was so happy to get a handful of candy, giving me smiles and hugs all around and welcoming me to Zimbabwe and asking for just a couple more pieces for their kids at home, that by the time I shook myself loose from all my new friends and got out to the vans, my guides had already distributed the ground operator's schedule for our next two days. Unfortunately, the timings on it bore little relationship to the ones on the sheet I had already given out to my guests. Not only that, but it listed among the highlights of our walk by the falls a hike down Devil's Cataract, which is about as safe for a group of sedentary American seniors as it sounds. "We don't do Devil's Cataract," I said, quickly confiscating the papers. Most of the passengers weren't upset, but one couple seemed quite disappointed that I wasn't going to allow them to risk being swept away by the world's most powerful falls.

So be a good colleague right from the beginning, and find out from the tour director what he's already told his group before giving out any information yourself, either verbally or in writing, and be flexible about the schedule.

The tour director and your listeners will also love you if you can be flexible about your commentary, especially if you work in a large country such as China, India, or the United States, and the group is flying from place to place, being led by different local guides for a couple of days in each area. For instance, if the tour director tells you a guide in one city already covered the basic history of the country or some other general national topic, stick to more local information.

On the other hand, if someone wants information about a subject, even if you intended to address it on some other day, go ahead and answer the question, and elaborate on the subject later as you had planned. Don't worry about repetition in that case. I'll never forget my first tour in Egypt, when one of my guests asked, "What's that growing out there in that field?" Staring straight ahead, our guide replied, "I talk about agriculture on Thursday."

Avoid speaking for your tour director. Imagine my surprise one day in South Africa when my guide suddenly said, "And now, I'm sure your tour director would like to take the mike and remind you about taking your malaria medications." I had intended to do no such thing. As far as I was concerned, the decision to take malaria meds or not is entirely a matter for the individual and his doctor. What if somebody who chose not to take them got upset at the implication that he had been given the wrong information back home? What if someone had a violent reaction to a medication my guide or I had urged him to take? It is not a can of worms I care to open.

This guide meant well. The last tour director she worked with had indeed taken the mike and given the group a lecture on the importance of taking their meds. But not all tour directors work the same way. Once again, communication is the key.

Best Friends Forever, at Least for a Few Days

You are a great resource for your tour director, because you know the territory better than he ever could. You have the local knowledge about things such as protocol or holiday traditions. You speak the local language. Your foreign colleague may not. The longer the tour, the more likely it is that a situation might arise when you can be of special service to him.

Protocol: I once led a two-week Stately Homes and Gardens tour of Ireland with a wonderful national guide named Marianne. Even though I had traveled extensively in the country independently, there was plenty about the culture I didn't know. I was familiar with Irish pubs and homey B&B accommodations. Protocol when visiting members of the nobility? Not so much.

Marianne gave me my first lesson in protocol when we visited the Earl and Countess of Rosse at their magnificent home, Birr Castle. She told me we needed to decide in advance who would sit on either side of the hosts at their respective tables at lunch in their formal dining room. The Earl had a long table, and the Countess had a round one. This was a rather intimidating idea to a democratically inclined American, so I was grateful for her guidance. We managed to figure it out, and the delicious lunch under the ancestral portraits was enjoyed by all, regardless of temporary rank assigned to the travelers. My feelings of intimidation vanished when the Earl, just back from Tibet and not yet unpacked, lifted one foot, pulled up his pants leg, and declared, "Jeeves wouldn't let Bertie Wooster wear these socks." When we left, the Countess gave me a book of photographs taken by her ancestor Mary, Countess of Rosse, a pioneering 19th-century photographer. These members of the nobility couldn't have been nicer or more down to earth!

However, I still had a bit of trepidation about the luncheon at our next estate, Baronscourt, home of the Duke and Duchess of Abercorn. A duke outranks an earl, and this duke was Northern Ireland's most senior peer. Maybe he'd be stuffier than the earl? The Duchess's Russian grandmother descended from the great poet Pushkin on one side and the

Romanovs on the other! Would she be proud and haughty? Marianne seemed more concerned about protocol this time, too. "Be sure to address them as "Your Grace," she warned us.

The great Georgian house had recently been redecorated by the esteemed British designer David Hicks, with intense red on the entry walls, salmon in the dining room, and blue and yellow down the hall. With all that playful color, the place was elegant, but certainly not stuffy. Nor were its noble inhabitants. The Duke showed us around, after asking, "Are all the ladies out of the loo? Do I have your permission to begin?" Being asked by the Duke if I had his permission to stroll about his own house relaxed me considerably, and I lost my nervousness completely when he said, "And here's where dear Dickie fell through the sofa!" ("Dear Dickie" was Lord Mountbatten.)

As we entered the dining room, the Duchess began telling me about the Pushkin Programme, a creative writing project for Irish children that she had recently founded, intended to promote peace and understanding between the North and the South. One of my guests joined in, eager as I was to hear about this wonderful work. The Duchess asked her to sit on her right at lunch, and me on her left, so that we could continue our conversation. I glanced frantically at Marianne, who signaled me that it was OK. "No protocol," she whispered. "It's a buffet."

So I sat next to the Duchess at lunch, remembered to call her Your Grace, and managed not to spill anything. *Thanks, Marianne!*

Holiday traditions: It was December 31st in the Galapagos, and my guests got a New Year's Eve to remember. We were on Santa Cruz Island, marveling at the giant tortoises that roam the highlands. At lunch, one of my guides, Celso, told me about Ecuador's *Año Viejo* tradition. In large cities and small villages alike, hundreds of life-sized effigies are burned in the streets at midnight, to symbolize the destruction of all that was negative in the old year. Political figures were very popular for this procedure, such as their president (and ours), along with pop-culture characters like Shrek.

We were anchored nearby for the night. Could we possibly see this? I didn't want my guests to miss such an opportunity, and I certainly didn't want to miss it myself. Celso agreed to escort us back onto the island that night after dinner for the celebration.

At 11:00, eight of us got into a Zodiac (called a *panga* in Ecuador) and docked at Puerto Ayora, Celso's home town. Dance music was blaring from a large open area by the waterfront. Bars were open and people were drinking beer in the streets, but amazingly, there was no rowdiness. It was festive and crowded, but a big family scene. Toddlers perched on their fathers' shoulders; teens gave their grandparents a supportive arm as everyone walked around laughing and talking, inspecting various effigies with loud approval. Celso took us through several back streets to see some special displays and introduced us to his friends. We felt like honorary locals.

At exactly midnight, all the effigies in the middle of the street were lit. Standing around one bonfire, we could see many others up and down the streets. Men held firecrackers flaming away in their hands and then tossed them into the pyre at the last minute. We all cheered and hugged and kissed and then took the *panga* back to our ship and drank Champagne. *Muchas gracias, Celso!*

Language: After touring the Peter and Paul Fortress in St. Petersburg, I steered my group to the toilets, where a scowling elderly Russian woman waited to collect ten rubles from me for each of my passengers. Eighteen women went in and came out, so I handed the *babushka* one hundred and eighty rubles. She started screaming at me and pointed toward the toilets. I shrugged, smiling weakly. In response, she screamed louder.

What was wrong? Did the *babushka* disagree with my count? Had one of my guests taken too much toilet paper? What in the world had I done to damage Russo-American relations? Thank heavens, just then my guide walked over.

"Oh," Nina said, "she's telling you that since you paid for the group, you can go in for free."

I had been hard at work for weeks learning Polite and Useful Phrases from my Russian phrasebook. *It's on me, honey; go ahead and take a free pee* was not one of them. *Spasibo, Nina!*

Tricky Questions: Sex, Religion, and Politics

As a local or national guide, the longer you travel with a group, the more likely you are to get into situations that a tour director routinely faces. Delicate topics can come up – sex, religion, or politics, for example. How do you handle them?

Sex: I think what you can get away with depends a lot on your gender. A male guide I worked with once in China had his passengers in stitches with his take on how much they were going to enjoy the foot massages. "Whenever we come here, I always hear a lot of *oooohh, aaaahh, oooohh, aaaahh!*" If I had moaned in simulated ecstasy on the mike, I would have gotten myself written up. Unfair, but that's how it is.

The furthest I've ever gone in that direction is when driving past Virgin's Leap Waterfall in Hohe Tauern National Park, Austria, on the many Alps tours I have led. The local legend says that one day a shepherdess was being pursued by a lusty shepherd. Rather than give in to his advances and lose her innocence, she leapt to her death. Miraculously, a beautiful waterfall sprang up from where she jumped.

I tell the story, pause a beat, and then say, "Personally, I think she made the wrong choice." And if there are teenagers on board, I don't even say that. The kids would giggle, but their parents might not.

On the other hand, some women can get away with anything a man can. Take my Irish friend Marianne. One day toward the end of our Stately Homes and Gardens tour, she held a limerick contest. I didn't compete, of course, but after a winner was chosen from among the guests' creations, I recited a limerick I had secretly written in her honor, in tribute to her comprehensive commentary.

There once was a National Guide,
With knowledge incredibly wide,
Who said, with a grin,
Once you let me begin,
I'll not stop till the end of the ride!

Then someone said, "Yes, Marianne, you do know everything about Ireland! But do you know any dirty limericks?"

Of course she did. And they loved it. I think the Irish accent definitely helped. Unfair, but that's how it is.

There once was a pair from Kildare,
Who tried to make love on the stair.
At the twenty-first stroke
The banister broke
So they finished it off in the air.

Incidentally, if you ever lead a tour in Amish country and drive through Intercourse, Pennsylvania, with a group of proper senior citizens who disapprove of four-letter words and would never dream of using them, be prepared for some surprisingly bawdy remarks! It was toward the end of the tour, and I guess they felt comfortable with me and each other by then.

Religion: If you're a born-again Christian or a militant atheist, keep it under your hat. Unless you are leading a pilgrimage or other exclusively religious tour made up entirely of co-religionists, treat religion as a cultural issue, not a personal one.

I once worked with a guide who was a devout Christian. When giving the day's schedule, he would add, "And then, Lord willing, we will go to lunch." Occasionally he would remark, "I thank the good Lord for the talents he has given me." Needless to say, this caused a fair amount of squirming in my group. He seemed to be just one step away from proselytizing. I had to ask not to work with him again.

At the opposite extreme, I was once a passenger on a trip to Turkey with a guide who was a confirmed secularist. He disdained religion and felt uncomfortable talking about it. Unfortunately, part of his job was to prepare the group for a visit to Konya and the Mevlana Museum. The building contains the tomb and shrine of Rumi, the great 12th-century poet, alongside the original lodge of the Mevlevi Whirling Dervishes, the mystical Sufi Muslim sect that Rumi founded.

On the coach ride to Konya, our guide said practically nothing about Rumi or the dervishes. When we arrived, he seemed to realize he ought to give his clients some sort of introduction, so he made us stand in the entryway of the shrine and talked for ten minutes while other groups passed us going in. Remember Rule #2: *Show-and-Tell Is for Grownups, Too?* He did not.

When we left, he said, "OK, I'll meet you at the exit in twenty minutes. It's by the gift shop." He pointed to the exit and was gone. Most of the other passengers trotted off to the gift shop and missed half the museum, which was in the other direction across the courtyard. It was full of fascinating dioramas and explanations about the dervishes. I raced through it and got to the shop just in time for our departure. The others were hanging around looking bored. Twenty minutes was too long for the shop and too short for the museum.

If he had abided by Rule #2 and done the commentary for the shrine on the coach and pointed out the rest of the museum at the beginning of our free time, our guide could have given us half an hour for both museum and shop. Unfortunately, his embarrassment about discussing religion disrupted his timing and short-changed the group.

You don't have to pretend to be a believer, if you aren't. When visiting religious sites, just describe them in neutral, factual terms. Even the non-believers in your group, or believers in a different religion, may well be fascinated by the rites and traditions of other faiths. Treat religion as you would any other aspect of your culture – a rich part of your heritage that people have traveled to see and learn about.

Politics: If you hold strong opinions about a current political situation, be careful how you share them with your clients. If you are asked about your own views concerning an upcoming election or other hot-button political issue, be a politician yourself. There are many creative ways to answer a question without really answering it, as all politicians know. Deflecting the question with a joke might help on occasion. Will Rogers, the great humorist, Cherokee cowboy, actor, writer, and one-time honorary mayor of Beverly Hills famously said, "I don't belong to any *organized* political party – I'm a Democrat."

If your country has been through political turmoil in your lifetime, you have a great opportunity to give your guests a balanced, first-person account of the transition. My wonderful Prague guide, Lucie, was nine years old when the Velvet Revolution occurred. As a kid, she thought Communism was wonderful, because her parents got free vacations to the seaside in Romania. Those summers were among her happiest childhood memories. However, now she was glad to live in a republic, she told me, because she was earning her MBA and figured that she would have a better chance to make a living under the current system.

Many of the guides I have worked with in Russia use humor to share what must have been painful transitions for themselves and their families. They often quote a common saying, *Life is better now, but we lived better then*, which sums it up for many of the older generation. *We pretended to work; they pretended to pay us* is another popular, wry description of the old order. Occasionally one of these sayings would inspire members of the group to ask questions about life in Russia then and now, which often led to some powerful and revealing discussions.

If you are willing to answer questions about how your country's past and current policies have affected your personal economics and those of your family members, you will have an eager audience. Your guests will feel like travelers, not just tourists.

Whenever you can involve your foreign visitors in the discussion, you will add another meaningful dimension to their trip. My American guests in Johannesburg were thrilled to hear from our guide, Louis, that pressure from the United States helped South Africa make the transition from apartheid to democracy. "If not for your support, Mandela would still be in prison." Louis added a personal note when he told us that under apartheid, blacks were on a waiting list for houses, which were given only to married couples. "We married for houses, and learned to love later." Even though he had a wife, Louis was on the waiting list for thirteen years. "Pressure from the United States helped to ease the laws in 1986 and I got a house. If not for you, I would still be on the list."

On a trip to China that I took many years ago, a national guide who called herself Candy was also generous in sharing her own experiences under her government's regulations. At twenty-nine, she explained, she was "the perfect age to talk about the New China, because I was so scared when I first saw foreigners. I didn't realize they were people, too."

Under the one-child policy in a society where males are overwhelmingly preferred, she told us, girl babies are often taken to orphanages, or meet a worse fate, so that the parents can try again for a boy. This has naturally created a huge gender imbalance in the country. If there are not enough women in one area, they can be sent to another. Candy grew up in Kunming but was "redistributed" to Guilin. At first she was assigned work as an English teacher but later was switched to guiding, her first choice. I found myself wondering how I would have handled being "redistributed." How would I have felt if I was told, after graduating from college, that I was off to a city over six hundred miles away, whether I wanted to move or not, to teach a subject I didn't care much about?

If you are passionate about a cause and wish to engage your clients in supporting it, don't proselytize. Don't beg them or annoy them. Inspire them instead, and time your pitch well. This is how it's done:

Tony, our ornithologist on an expedition cruise of Antarctica and the Falklands, was passionately dedicated to seabirds, especially the Wandering Albatross. Tall and lanky, he strongly resembled one himself. His lectures were brilliant. Tony was knowledgeable, funny, and tirelessly devoted to our education about "these magnificent seabirds." One evening he came running into the dining room, flapping his long arms with excitement, and dragged us out onto the deck to see an albatross that had begun following the ship. It was indeed a magnificent sight. We all fell in love with Tony and his seabirds.

Late in the cruise, he gave us a sobering slide lecture called "Getting Seabirds off the Hook." He showed us how thousands of birds around the world were being drowned every year, caught on baited hooks laid by long-line fishing vessels. The great albatrosses in particular were endangered by this fishing method. In fact, scientists were concerned that if legal measures were not introduced to prevent this by-catch, several species of albatross could become extinct in the next few years.

We were all distressed. "Tony, that's terrible! What can we do to help save them?"

Tony was ready for that reaction. He thanked us for our concern and asked if he could give us a sample letter to send to our members of Congress to urge the United States to sign a new international treaty with an action plan to reduce seabird mortality. Everyone took a copy of Tony's *Save the Albatross Campaign* letter, and I'm sure most of us sent them off as soon as we returned home. I know I did. How could we not? Tony had gotten us completely hooked on seabirds!

And Louis, our Jo'burg guide? His passion was literacy. "Education is everything, but we don't read," he said, sadly. When pointing out St. John's School on our tour, he told us, "Every parent in Soweto would like to send his kid here." Unfortunately, there are not enough schools to meet the demand, they are expensive and, due to the legacy of apartheid, many black students are not ready for higher education. "Sixty percent of our black teachers have not been to university."

So Louis is doing something about it. Together with a group of neighborhood teens, he built a community youth center. It began as a gathering place for young people to come and talk to an adult about what was on their minds, to sing and to dance. Gradually, a troupe was formed, and tour groups began visiting the center to watch these gifted young people perform.

Louis's example of volunteerism and his tireless advocacy for literacy inspired a couple of tour director colleagues of mine to suggest that their guests bring children's books with them to South Africa and help him build a library. We all spread the word about the project, and the center now houses thousands of books, brought in a few at a time by visitors inspired by Louis to help create a special place for reading in Soweto. The kids built the shelves. Louis serves as librarian and custodian. "It's made such a difference in the community," he reports.

It's made a difference for all of us who donated books, too. We feel connected to the lovely young people who performed for us. We feel invested in their future. Louis, a great guide, welcomed us into his community, allowed us to participate in their lives, and turned our trip into a journey.

11

EPILOGUE

———

Travel Is Fatal to Prejudice, Bigotry, and Narrow-Mindedness (Mark Twain)

I don't think it's overstating the case to say that a great guide can be a powerful cultural ambassador – a tiny but vital force toward the goal of international understanding and peace among nations.

Americans and many others around the world will never forget the events of September 11, 2001. Russia faced its own unthinkable tragedy nearly three years later, when Chechen militants invaded School Number One in Beslan, in the Russian Caucasus, on September 1, 2004. It was the first day of the school year, known as Knowledge Day. A festive, joyous celebration turned into a terrifying three-day siege, ending with explosions, fire, and a fierce gun battle between Russian security forces and the terrorists. Over 1,100 hostages were taken and more than 300 were killed. Nearly two-thirds of them were schoolchildren.

When the siege began, I was with an American group on the train from Moscow to St. Petersburg. We heard the news when we arrived late that night. For the next two days, our local guide and driver mastered their emotions and managed to lead us through the usual St. Petersburg program of sightseeing, despite the alarming news updates we kept hearing. Our guide, Svetlana, reassured my nervous guests that they themselves were in no danger from the terrorists. She kept everyone occupied and distracted as cheerfully as anyone possibly could have.

On the final day of the siege, when the full horrors of the massacre became known, we were en route to Peterhof Palace, with a stop to visit the beautiful Moorish-style Grand Choral Synagogue. All of Russia was in shock and mourning.

My American guests knew that the Beslan tragedy was Russia's 9/11, and their empathy was obvious. We all wanted to show our concern. One of my Jewish guests approached me and asked if he could lead us in the Kaddish, the Hebrew prayer for the dead, during our synagogue visit. I spoke with Svetlana, who readily agreed to ask the cantor.

When we arrived, the normally genial cantor was ashen and somber, and the usually cheery custodian was shaking with uncontrollable sobbing. But Svetlana, although she was just as devastated as the others, kept it all together. She taught us a few words of condolence in Russian, which we whispered to the custodian as we hugged her. Svetlana then asked the cantor if an American might lead everyone in prayer.

As my guest spoke the Mourner's Kaddish in memory of those precious children, their teachers, and their parents, we all stood together – Jew, Gentile, non-believer, Russian, American – silently paying our respects, each in his own way. The Kaddish does not mention death; it is above all a prayer for peace. In that moment, there were no divisions, just empathy, sorrow, and love.

Svetlana's courage and calm professionalism helped us all to get through that day and brought Russians and Americans together in a profound emotional connection. She remains an inspiration to me and a shining example to us all.

Does international travel help lead to understanding between cultures? I'm sure every thoughtful traveler will agree that it does. Can cultural exchange ultimately guide us to a more peaceful global society? We can hope so. Certainly the great guides of the world can begin to lead us all in the right direction.

ACKNOWLEDGEMENTS

———

To all the guides I've ever traveled with, thank you for the inspiration. You have enriched my life more than you will ever know, and I am eternally grateful for everything that you have shown me.

To my fellow tour directors – mentors all – my deepest gratitude. I can't possibly name all the tour directors I have learned from, but you know who you are. I must credit Tris Tirol with the Virgin's Leap joke, and I would be remiss if I didn't single out my earliest mentors for their generosity of spirit. Therefore, I owe a special debt of gratitude to Cherie Anderson, Mary Harold, and of course the amazing ITMI team: Ted Bravos, Joanne Connors, and Randy Hellrung.

Heartfelt thanks to Tauck, Academic Arrangements Abroad, AFC Vacations, Explore America, Architours, and all the other fine travel companies that have entrusted me with their valuable clients all over the globe. At Tauck, I am particularly grateful to Marianna Cornelius, Steve Jobrack, Kristen Mack, Jacque Moran, Corry Soetens, and Kendra St. John. At Academic Arrangements Abroad, special thanks go to Harriet Friedlander and Jim Friedlander.

I am most grateful to Kate Benzin, Alice K. Boatwright, Jane Jacobs, Dianne Synder, Heidi Wilson, and Laura Zweig for carefully reading an early draft of the manuscript and for their invaluable editorial comments and suggestions. Any errors that remain are, of course, my own. I would also like to thank David Rosenbloom and Jack Salem for sharing with me their own journeys through the publishing maze.

When I was eleven years old, my father, Keith Wilson, came bounding down the stairs of our New Haven home one afternoon singing, "California, here we come!" A professor of music at Yale University, he had just been notified of an appointment on the faculty of UCLA for the summer. He and my mother, Rachel, decided it would be "educational" to show their kids as much of the country as possible on the way from Connecticut to California and back. They piled me and my sisters, Laura, Heidi, and Holly, into the family station wagon, and we were off on a road trip that for me has never ended. Thanks, Dad!

My husband, Jon Harvey, has provided unwavering emotional support, expert advice, delicious dinners, and heavenly backrubs throughout this project. For all that, there can never be enough thanks.

Made in the USA
San Bernardino, CA
24 June 2014